WORLD
HISTORY SERIES ■■■

The Age of Feudalism

by
Timothy Levi Biel

Lucent Books, P.O. Box 289011, San Diego, CA 92198-9011

Titles in the World History Series

The Age of Feudalism   The Hundred Years' War
Ancient Greece   The Roman Empire
The French and Indian War   The Roman Republic
Hitler's Reich   The Russian Revolution

Library of Congress Cataloging-in-Publication Data

Biel, Timothy L.
    The age of feudalism / by Timothy L. Biel.
       p. cm.—(World history series)
    Includes bibliographical references and index.
    Summary: Discusses feudalism, the system of government based on ownership of land, as it was practiced in Europe in the Middle Ages.
    ISBN 1-56006-232-0
    1. Feudalism—Juvenile literature. 2. Europe—Politics and government—476–1492—Juvenile literature. [1. Feudalism. 2. Europe—History—476–1492.] I. Title. II. Series.
D131.B46   1994
321'.3—dc20   93-19290
                                  CIP
                                  AC

Foreword

Each year on the first day of school, nearly every history teacher faces the task of explaining why his or her students should study history. One logical answer to this question is that exploring what happened in our past explains how the things we often take for granted—our customs, ideas, and institutions—came to be. As statesman and historian Winston Churchill put it, "Every nation or group of nations has its own tale to tell. Knowledge of the trials and struggles is necessary to all who would comprehend the problems, perils, challenges, and opportunities which confront us today." Thus, a study of history puts modern ideas and institutions in perspective. For example, though the founders of the United States were talented and creative thinkers, they clearly did not invent the concept of democracy. Instead, they adapted some democratic ideas that had originated in ancient Greece and with which the Romans, the British, and others had experimented. An exploration of these cultures, then, reveals their very real connection to us through institutions that continue to shape our daily lives.

Another reason often given for studying history is the idea that lessons exist in the past from which contemporary societies can benefit and learn. This idea, although controversial, has always been an intriguing one for historians. Those who agree that society can benefit from the past often quote philosopher George Santayana's famous statement, "Those who cannot remember the past are condemned to repeat it." Historians who ascribe to Santayana's philosophy believe that, for example, studying the events that led up to the major world wars or other significant historical events would allow society to chart a different and more favorable course in the future.

Just as difficult as convincing students to realize the importance of studying history is the search for useful and interesting supplementary materials that present historical events in a context that can be easily understood. The volumes in Lucent Books' World History Series attempt to present a broad, balanced, and penetrating view of the march of history. Ancient Egypt's important wars and rulers, for example, are presented against the rich and colorful backdrop of Egyptian religious, social, and cultural developments. The series engages the reader by enhancing historical events with these cultural contexts. For example, in *Ancient Greece*, the text covers the role of women in that society. Slavery is discussed in *The Roman Empire*, as well as how slaves earned their freedom. The numerous and varied aspects of everyday life in these and other societies are explored in each volume of the series. Additionally, the series covers the major political, cultural, and philosophical ideas as the torch of civilization is passed from ancient Mesopotamia and Egypt, through Greece, Rome, Medieval Europe, and other world cultures, to the modern day.

The material in the series is formatted in a thorough, precise, and organized manner. Each volume offers the reader a comprehensive and clearly written overview of an important historical event or period. The topic under discussion is placed in a broad, historical context. For example, *The Italian Renaissance* begins with a discussion of the High Middle Ages and the loss of central control that allowed certain Italian cities to develop artistically. The book ends by looking forward to the Reformation and interpreting the societal changes that grew out of the Renaissance. Thus, students are not only involved in an historical era, but also enveloped by the events leading up to that era and the events following it.

One important and unique feature in the World History Series is the primary and secondary source quotations that richly supplement each volume. These quotes are useful in a number of ways. First, they allow students access to sources they would not normally be exposed to because of the difficulty and obscurity of the original source. The quotations range from interesting anecdotes to far-sighted cultural perspectives and are drawn from historical witnesses both past and present. Second, the quotes demonstrate how and where historians themselves derive their information on the past as they strive to reach a consensus on historical events. Lastly, all of the quotes are footnoted, familiarizing students with the citation process and allowing them to verify quotes and/or look up the original source if the quote piques their interest.

Finally, the books in the World History Series provide a detailed launching point for further research. Each book contains a bibliography specifically geared toward student research. A second, annotated bibliography introduces students to all the sources the author consulted when compiling the book. A chronology of important dates gives students an overview, at a glance, of the topic covered. Where applicable, a glossary of terms is included.

In short, the series is designed not only to acquaint readers with the basics of history, but also to make them aware that their lives are a part of an ongoing human saga. Perhaps they will then come to the same realization as famed historian Arnold Toynbee. In his monumental work, *A Study of History,* he wrote about becoming aware of history flowing through him in a mighty current, and of his own life "welling like a wave in the flow of this vast tide."

Important Dates in the Age of Feudalism

A.D. 450	500	550	600	650	700	750	800	850	900

476
Sack of Rome brings an end to the Western Roman Empire

481
Clovis and the Franks begin conquest of France

751–768
Pepin the Short rules Franks

756
Donation of Pepin establishes political power of the church

768–814
Reign of Charlemagne as king of the Franks

800
Pope Leo III crowns Charlemagne emperor of the Holy Roman Empire

814–840
Reign of Louis the Pious as king of the Franks

841–924
Norse raids in France

843–873
Louis's sons, Louis the German, Charles the Bald, and Lothar agree to the Partition of Verdun, which divides Charlemagne's empire into three

911
Rollo becomes first duke of Normandy

987–996
Reign of Hugh Capet, king of France, founder of Capetian dynasty of French monarchs

1042–1066
Reign of Edward the Confessor, king of England

1066
Battle of Hastings; King Harold of England killed; England conquered by the Normans

1066–1087
Reign of William I, king of England

1073–1085
Pontificate of Gregory VII

1076
Pope Gregory VII excommunicates Henry IV, the German emperor

1085
The Domesday Book of King William I is completed

1095
Pope Urban II proclaims the First Crusade

1099
Crusaders take Jerusalem

1099–1143
Duration of the Latin Kingdom of Jerusalem

1100–1135
Reign of Henry I, king of England

950	1000	1050	1100	1150	1200	1250	1300	1350

1108–1137
Reign of Louis VI,
king of France

1135–1154
Reign of Stephen,
king of England

1137–1180
Reign of Louis VII,
king of France

1146–1148
Second Crusade

1154–1189
Reign of Henry II,
king of England

1180–1223
Reign of Philip II,
Augustus, king of France

1189–1192
Third Crusade

1189–1199
Reign of Richard I,
the Lion-hearted,
king of England

1199–1216
Reign of John,
king of England

1202–1204
Fourth Crusade

1202–1205
French king, Philip II,
takes Normandy, Anjou,
Maine, and Brittany
from England

1204
Crusaders sack
Constantinople

1214
King Philip II defeats
King John at Bouvines,
drives English from
France for good

1215
Magna Carta; English
barons gain concessions
from King John

1216–1272
Reign of Henry III,
king of England

1226–1270
Reign of Louis IX,
St. Louis, king of France

1272–1307
Reign of Edward I,
king of England

1295
Edward I forms Model
Parliament

1302
French king, Philip IV,
forms first Estates General

Feudalism: The Birth of the Middle Ages

In the Middle Ages, during the period of European history between approximately 800 and 1350, knights, or mounted soldiers, were the most important members of the military. By the year 1000, they also formed the majority of the nobility, or ruling class in Europe. Their authority to rule was based on the amount of land they owned. Whoever held the land ruled it. This was the essence of feudalism, the system of private government and military organization that prevailed during the Middle Ages throughout England and in the regions of Europe we now call France, Belgium, Luxembourg, the Netherlands, Germany, Austria, Switzerland, and Italy.

Knights engage in the sport of jousting. Jousting and other martial sports provided a way for these professional soldiers to win honors and property outside of war.

A Time of Change

The Middle Ages was a period of great change. Classical Roman civilization had virtually disappeared, and modern Western civilization was just emerging. Feudalism was a vital factor in the formation of this new civilization. But like the civilization it helped to form, feudalism was constantly changing and evolving. By the time it had fully developed into a system of government, it was already being replaced by powerful monarchies and leagues of city governments throughout Europe. By the time the majority of knights had made the climb in social status from elite soldiers to members of the ruling class, the richest and strongest of them were beginning to control most of the political power.

A vassal kneels before his lord and swears his loyalty. The vassal was entitled to a fief as long as he served the lord faithfully.

The Feudal Oath

Nevertheless, feudalism in medieval Europe developed an economic, military, and government system that has never been duplicated in any other time or place in the world. It was based on contracts, or feudal oaths, between lords and vassals. A vassal was usually a knight. The core of this oath was the vassal's promise of loyalty and military service to his superior, or lord. In return, the lord granted his vassal a fee, or gift. The Latin word for this fee, which was used in most official ceremonies and documents well into the tenth century, was *feudum,* which is where the word *feudalism* comes from. In France and England, the feudum or fee became known as a fief.

The earliest fiefs given to vassals by their lords were gifts such as armor, weapons, or horses. By the year 1000, the typical fief had become a parcel of land, which the vassal was entitled to hold as long as he lived and as long as he continued to serve his lord faithfully. The vassal was also entitled to rule all people who lived on his land and to take from the land all profits he deemed to be appropriate. That is how knights gradually rose in status from rich, elite soldiers to wealthy members of the ruling class. And it is how the feudal oath, normally called an oath of homage during the Middle Ages, evolved from a solemn vow of military loyalty into a political tool for acquiring land and power.

The size of each vassal's fief varied greatly. The kings of France and England, for example, divided their entire kingdoms into fifty or sixty fiefs, each of which was granted to a vassal. These vassals became the great lords of France and England. In France they were dukes and counts. In England, they were usually called dukes or earls. A great lord was expected to supply his king with a great army of knights, sometimes as many as several hundred, whenever called upon.

Kingdoms Divided into Fiefs

To meet their fealty, or feudal obligations to a king, the great lords divided, or subinfeudated, their duchies, counties, and earldoms among vassals of their own. Even the fiefs of these rear vassals were too large for a single person to manage, so they were further divided or subinfeudated until the lowest ranking vassal in the chain of ownership held a fief that consisted of a single peasant village and about a hundred acres of farmland.

Ultimately most of northern Europe was divided in this manner. Kingdoms were divided into duchies, counties, or earldoms, which were subdivided into smaller fiefs, and these fiefs were further divided and subdivided. Eventually, all vassals, no matter how small their fiefs, were considered members of the nobility. Although many usually had no vassals of their own, they were still lords over all the peasants who lived on their land, and they had almost total control over the lives and welfare of these peasants.

Feudalism organized society during a violent and lawless time after the fall of the Roman Empire. It developed into a system of government and law that gave rise to the great civilizations and empires of Western Europe. That is what makes feudalism such a fascinating and important part of Western history. It helped European civilization lift itself out of the Dark Ages. At the same time, it helped restore much of the classic art, learning, and technology of ancient Rome. To this day we admire the achievements of the Middle Ages: the founding of universities; the renewal of theology, philosophy, and law; the flowering of

Peasant farmers, or serfs, work the land surrounding their lord's castle. In return for their labor, the lord protected them.

literature and art; the splendor of royal palaces; and the architectural grandeur of medieval cathedrals. Feudalism helped to make the Western world civilized again after several centuries of decline, and it all began with the knights, who were soldiers and politicians on horseback.

The Forerunners of Feudalism

In A.D. 98, the Roman historian Tacitus wrote about the northern colonies of the Roman Empire near the Rhine River in what is now western Germany. In Roman times, the Rhine separated Roman civilization from the "barbarians," or non-Romans. Tacitus was intrigued by the barbarian tribes, and he wrote about several such groups, which he called the Germanic tribes.

Tacitus was most fascinated by the Germanic tribes' bands of elite warriors, which he called *comitatus*. The *comites*, or members of the bands, swore unswerving loyalty to their leaders, or chieftains. In return, whenever a tribe was victorious in battle, the chieftain rewarded members generously with booty, or objects taken from the victims. Comites were prestigious members of their tribes. When a chieftain died, his successor was usually chosen from the comitatus. In the following passage, Tacitus describes the obligations and rewards of being a warrior in a Germanic comitatus:

> It brings fame and glory to a leader not only in his own folk, but among neighboring peoples, if his warband is superior in numbers and courage.
>
> When they go to war it is a disgrace for the chief to be outdone in deeds of valor, and for the followers not to equal the courage of their chief. Moreover, for a follower to survive his chief and come unharmed out of a battle is life-long infamy and shame. . . . The chief fights for victory, the men for their chief. . . .
>
> They depend on their chief for their war-horse, and their weapons; they consider their [minimum] pay to be the feasts [which he provides], but the real wealth [which attracts them] comes from war and plunder.[1]

The comitatus was the organization that would later develop into a system of feudal lords and vassals. Like vassals, members of the comitatus fought for their leader and for glory. To be slain on the battlefield was far more desirable to them than to survive a battle in which one's chief was slain.

Because these barbarian warriors were fierce and fearless soldiers who seemed to live for the glory of battle, the Romans recruited many of them into their armies. In fact, by A.D. 300, more Germanic soldiers than Romans fought in the Roman army. Even many of the generals were Germanic, and many of them selected elite soldiers to form their own private armies, similar to the Germanic comitatus.

In about 400, warlike Huns from central Asia pushed into Europe, beginning a great westward migration of the Germanic

A Germanic tribe. The Romans called them barbarians, but their tribal organization, centered around a chief, formed the basis of feudal society.

tribes into the Roman Empire. Historians have identified several Germanic tribes that migrated into the Roman Empire in the fifth century. From western Germany came the Franks, the Angles, and the Saxons. From eastern Germany came the Goths, the Vandals, the Burgundians, and the Lombards.

The End of Roman Civilization

Within seventy-five years, the invading Germanic tribes brought an end to Roman civilization. The Franks established their kingdom in the area the Romans called Gaul, where France is now located. The period that followed, from 500 to 800, is often called the Dark Ages. Unlike the literate Greco-Roman culture that had dominated Europe for more than a thousand years, the Germanic culture had no written language. Much of the learning, the science, and the technology of the earlier civilizations was lost. What small collections of Roman literature were not destroyed were harbored in a handful of monasteries throughout Europe. The only remaining link to Roman civilization was the Roman church, which retained the Latin language and some elements of the Roman law and hierarchy, or chain of command.

Two Gauls, members of the Germanic tribe that settled in present-day France.

Although the culture the barbarian tribes brought to Gaul was not as literary, or as technically advanced as Roman civilization had been, the Germanic tribes did not destroy Roman civilization. The empire had decayed from within, and the tribes that invaded Europe in the fifth and sixth centuries introduced a new way of life to replace the culture that was dying. In fact, many of the Germanic chieftains greatly admired the Romans and tried to preserve many Roman customs. Out of the marriage of new Germanic customs with old Roman customs, feudalism was born.

1 The First Kings

After Clovis, king of the Franks, had conquered all of the Frankish tribes, he set up a government modeled on the Roman Catholic church.

Around the year 500, the most powerful Frankish chieftain was Clovis, whose name meant "battle of glory." Clovis was a great admirer of the Romans. He created cavalries of mounted soldiers like the Romans. He adopted Roman-style mail armor. He was also deeply impressed by the monasteries that remained in the old Roman colonies and by the wisdom of the churchmen who lived in them.

In 496 Clovis converted to Christianity, and his conversion helped to shape the political future of Europe. With his mounted soldiers, Clovis conquered almost all the other Frankish chieftains and forced them and their subjects to become Christian. Clovis assumed the Latin title *rex,* or king, and he declared himself king of the Frankish people. To this day, French school children are taught that Clovis was the first king of France. In French his name is Louis I.

The Rise of the Frankish Counts

The Christianizing of the Franks made them allies of the Roman church. More important, Clovis applied Roman laws and customs to the Franks, establishing throughout his kingdom a hierarchy modeled after that of the Roman church. Just as the church

Frankish chiefs meet with a Roman general. Roman influence had existed in Gaul for centuries before Clovis.

divided its authority regionally among bishops, Clovis divided his kingdom among his most powerful comites. Over the years, the term evolved to the French *comte,* or "count," and the land over which a comte ruled became known as his *comté,* or "county."

Despite having adopted numerous Roman customs, the Franks retained many Germanic traditions. For example, they were not accustomed to obeying a strong king, especially in peacetime. In the Germanic tradition, a king was merely the most powerful of the chieftains, who came forward to lead his people in time of war. When a Germanic "king" died, his land was divided among his sons. Accordingly, before Clovis died, he divided his kingdom among his three sons. They all kept the title of king, but by the time the sons of Clovis had divided their "kingdoms" among their own sons, these third-generation "kings" had no more power than the descendants of Clovis's counts.

For the next two centuries, most counts ignored these weak kings. They assembled their own private cavalries of knights, but since no clear laws or established government protected individual property rights, they fought amongst themselves for control of the land. Anyone who did not have a strong cavalry lost his land to a more powerful count. Many freemen, or small landowners, were forced to commend themselves, or give up their land to a count who was willing to offer them protection from other counts.

The counts often required their commended subjects to swear an oath of loyalty before a monk, because monks were among the few people who could read and write, hence were able to record these promises. Latin was used instead of the Frankish language, for which there was still no written version. The following example, translated from a medieval book of "Formulas," was a standard oath of commendation in the first half of the seventh century:

> You have been willing to allow me to hand myself over or commend myself to your protection. This I have done on these conditions: You are to aid and support me with food and clothing, insofar as I shall be able to serve you and deserve well of you. As long as I shall live, I am bound to give you service and obedience. . . . For the rest of my life I shall have no power to withdraw from your lordship and protection, but all the days of my life I must remain under your power and defense.[2]

The Earliest Feudal Oaths

Many of the Frankish counts began to demand similar oaths of their knights. In addition to his lifelong loyalty, the knight promised to give his lord regular military service. In this special oath, called an oath of homage, the soldier was usually referred to as a *fidelis,* which is Latin for "faithful man" or "vassal," and the count was referred to as the "lord." This example of one of the earliest formulas for a feudal oath, or oath of homage, was written in the eighth century:

> It is right that those who promise us unbroken faith should be placed under our protection. And because [*so-and-so*], our *fidelis,* has come here in our palace with his weapons, and has sworn, in our hand, loyalty and fidelity, therefore, by this present document, we decree and order that from now on he be considered one of our vassals.[3]

By the year 700, becoming a vassal and swearing homage to a lord was the custom for all knights, who enjoyed increases in wealth and social status as a result. A lord usually offered his knights armor, horses, fine clothing, a home at the castle, or sometimes the produce from a small piece of land. Some of the most prized knights were granted land outright. Such a gift was called a benefice, or sometimes a *precarium.* The knight's possession of this land was, indeed, precarious. It was understood that if he did not fulfill his duties, the count would take the land back. When the knight died, the land was returned to the count.

This was the state of politics in Europe during the Dark Ages. There was no government except the rule of a count over his lands. Counts had no written laws to follow, so most judgments and punishments of crimes were based on local customs and ancient Germanic traditions of revenge. Private property was safe only in proportion to the owner's ability to defend it.

Pepin the Short: The First Strong Frankish King

Around the year 740, one particularly powerful Frankish count called Pepin the Short threatened to attack other counts unless they swore homage to him. Many complied, and Pepin demanded that each count supply him with a number of knights. Pepin led this great army against other Germanic tribes, especially the Lombards, who had settled in Italy. The Lombards were still non-Christian and therefore enemies of the Roman church.

When Pepin succeeded in driving the Lombards from Rome, he not only expanded the influence of the Franks, he also gained an important ally—the church. He donated to the pope a strip of the land he had captured in Italy. A small piece of this so-called Donation of Pepin remains in church hands to this day. It is the Vatican, an independent state governed by the Roman Catholic church. This was the beginning of the church's secular, or nonreligious power,

Pope Stephen II proclaims Pepin king of the Franks in 754. Pepin's gift of land to the pope set the stage for the church's great political influence in Europe.

The Reign of Charlemagne

The series of kings established by Pepin is known today as the Carolingian line. Its name is derived from that of the most famous of the Carolingian kings, Pepin's son Charles, later called Charlemagne, who was born in 742. Charlemagne, with his head of long, golden hair, was a giant among men, physically, politically, and philosophically. At a time when the height of the average European male was a little over five feet, Charlemagne, standing six feet four inches tall, towered over most of his contemporaries.

Mounted on horseback and decked in armor, the Frankish ruler must have cast an extraordinary presence. That may have helped him in his many military campaigns. Charlemagne reigned as king of the Franks for almost half a century, from 768 to 814. In the first thirty-four years of his reign, he led fifty-three military campaigns. He defended Italy from the raiding Saracens and turned back the Moors in northern Spain. He conquered and Christianized the Germanic kingdoms of Saxony and Bavaria.

Pepin's son Charlemagne, or Charles the Great, became the first emperor of the Holy Roman Empire on Christmas Day, A.D. 800.

which would continue to grow until the church had become one of the most powerful political forces in medieval Europe. In gratitude, Pope Stephen proclaimed the Frankish leader Pepin III, king of Frankland. Thus Pepin established a line of Frankish kings, who would contribute greatly to the history of Europe and to the evolution of feudalism.

The Founding of the Holy Roman Empire

By 800, Charlemagne's empire was nearly as large as the classical Roman Empire had been. It stretched from Italy in the south to what is now northern Germany in the north, across all of modern-day France and most of modern Germany, Austria, Czechoslovakia, and Hungary. In the year 800, Pope Leo III honored Charlemagne by declaring the lands under his rule the new Roman Empire. And in a Christmas Day ceremony at St. Peter's Basilica in Rome, Leo crowned Charlemagne "Charles Augustus, emperor of the Romans."

Charlemagne viewed his domain, now known as the Holy Roman Empire, as an extension of the original Roman Empire. He viewed his conquests of the Saxons, Burgundians, Bavarians, and Lombards, as well as his unsuccessful campaign to drive the Muslims out of Spain, as his Christian duty. And, as he had stated in a letter to Leo in 796, he believed that the pope's duty was to pray for the success of Charlemagne:

> Your task, most holy father, is to lift up your hands to God, like Moses, so as to aid our troops, so that through your intercession the Christian people may, with God as its leader and giver of victory, always and everywhere be victori-

This illumination from an ancient manuscript depicts Pope Leo III crowning Charlemagne emperor at Saint Peter's in Rome.

ous over the enemies of His Holy Name, and so that the name of Our Lord Jesus Christ may be famous throughout the world.[4]

Most of the conquered Saxon and Bavarian tribes still worshiped traditional pagan gods. Charlemagne gave them a choice: Christianity or death. On one Christmas Eve, he had 4,500 Saxon rebels beheaded for refusing baptism. Later that same night, he went to mass and celebrated the birth of Jesus.

The Revival of Learning Under Charlemagne

Though ruthless in his zeal to spread both Christianity and his empire, Charlemagne possessed a remarkable intellect, which he applied to his goal of re-creating the classical Roman Empire in the midst of barbarians. An able scholar, Charlemagne was fluent in Latin and could understand Greek. He was apparently fond of quoting from scripture or from the classic Latin authors such as Virgil. In fact, Charlemagne demanded that the monks in monasteries throughout his kingdom make good, accurate copies of the Bible and all the Latin literature they could find. We are indebted to Charlemagne for preserving the manuscripts of almost all the classics of Latin literature. Much of what we know about the classical Roman Empire today would have been lost if not for this medieval king.

Charlemagne traveled to Constantinople, capital of the Byzantine Empire, and he built grand palaces and cathedrals throughout his own realm to imitate those he had seen abroad. Perhaps the grandest learning, technology, and government. He knew that literacy and learning were essential to the civilization he dreamed of. Therefore he charged the church with the responsibility of educating all his subjects—not just the counts and their deputies, but all his subjects. In 787 Charlemagne ordered that "every cathedral and monastery in the kingdom establish schools" so that even the poorest of his subjects could become literate: "Take care to make no difference between the sons of serfs and of freemen, so that they might come and sit on the same benches to study grammar, music, and arithmetic."[6]

The Aachen cathedral, destroyed in World War II, was originally built by Charlemagne in the ninth century to serve as his capital city's church.

Charlemagne presides over the palace school at his Aachen palace. During his reign he brought order, literacy, and centralized government to most of Europe.

of these were the palace and cathedral in Aachen, the northern German city he established as his capital. Both stood for more than a thousand years, before they were destroyed by bombs in World War II. According to written descriptions by Einhard, Charlemagne's secretary and biographer, the palace featured a circular dome and, inside, a two-story circular colonnade. It was, says Einhard, "adorned with gold and silver and lamps, railings and doors of bronze, a famous mosaic, and crucibles brought from Rome and Ravenna."[5]

Charlemagne sought to restore the greatness of the Roman Empire in the West, not only in imperial splendor, but in

A System of Government Emerges

The government Charlemagne established represented a mixture of his native Germanic customs and the Roman models he had studied. Like his father and the Frankish kings before him, he used feudal oaths as the basis for building the support of the Frankish counts and their vassals. Most newly conquered land he divided among these vassals, the *fideles,* as shown by this entry from his annals, or yearly records:

> Vast numbers of Saxons were deported, together with their wives and children, to various parts of the kingdom. The land from which they had been removed was distributed by the king among his faithful men (*fideles*), that is to say among his bishops, priests, counts, and other vassals.[7]

Charlemagne made one important change in the responsibilities of his vassals.

Under Pepin and other Frankish kings, the counts had remained extremely independent. They had but one obligation to their king—to answer his summons to arms. Charlemagne, on the other hand, demanded that his counts and other vassals appear at a general assembly at least once a year to hold court and offer their opinions on matters of law. He used these general assemblies to help build a central government and to solidify his control over the nobility.

At the assemblies, nobles deliberated on the king's proposals for taxes, for punishing crimes, for penalizing vassals who deserted their lords, and so forth. They submitted suggestions to Charlemagne, who considered these ideas and then formulated laws, or *capitula.* Sixty-five capitularies, or written collections of Charlemagne's capitula, have been preserved. They are perhaps the greatest legacy of Charlemagne's government.

The capitularies were the first written code of law to replace traditional Germanic customs. In reality, many of the capitularies

This illustration from a fourteenth-century manuscript depicts Charlemagne receiving a feudal oath from one of his vassals.

were merely written extensions of these customs. For example, they endorsed the archaic traditions of trial by ordeal, in which a person accused of a crime had to prove his innocence by withstanding flames or surviving being tossed, with feet and hands

A medieval bishop. From Charlemagne's time on, bishops exercised great influence in temporal affairs.

bound, into a river. The capitularies also retained trial by combat, in which accused and accuser would battle to the death.

Despite the preservation of some of these crude customs, Charlemagne's capitularies were a noble attempt to transform a barbarian society into a civilized one, and they display an astonishing grasp of systematic government. Some capitula helped to encourage trade and commerce. They regulated weights, measures, and money. They protected fairs, moderated tolls, and established taxes for the building of roads and bridges. They even set up a state welfare system.

To monitor the effectiveness of his government, Charlemagne assigned special envoys, or representatives, to investigate all the counties in his empire. These envoys were important and trusted aides to the king. If they observed anything amiss in the counties—a vassal who was ignoring the king's capitula, abusing his authority or using excessive punishment, or not collecting or paying enough taxes—the envoys summoned a group of leading citizens of the county to hear evidence and give a sworn statement, or verdict, condemning or acquitting the accused party. These were the crude beginnings of trial by jury.

The Rise of an Elite Noble Class

By these means Charlemagne established a central government. Along with his counts, he entrusted a great deal of power to the church, specifically to the bishops. Nearly every count had to share his authority with a bishop. Technically, the

An idealized painting of Charlemagne as a powerful warrior-king. The great ruler nearly single-handedly moved Europe out of the Dark Ages.

bishop was in charge of church or sacred affairs, while the count was responsible for secular or nonsacred affairs. In practice, the two officials ruled together. It was often difficult to tell where the bishop's authority left off and the count's began. The balance between counts and bishops helped keep both the nobility and the church from taking too much control, especially since Charlemagne firmly guarded his right to appoint both counts and bishops.

Charlemagne also assigned a handful of his most trusted vassals greater power than the rest. These vassals were usually given the title of duke or marquis, and along with the title they received "great commands" over several counties. Many counts resented being commanded by dukes, and occasionally a discontented count would call his vassals to war against an overbearing duke.

During the time of Charlemagne, however, relations among the nobility appear to have been quite harmonious, especially compared to later centuries. A duke seldom interfered with a count's rule except to make certain that the count met his military and judicial obligations. To ensure that he was in fact able to meet these obligations and to help him rule his county, a count usually had to have numerous vassals of his own. The most powerful of these were the viscounts, or deputy counts. Typically, a viscount was given a district within the county as his fief, and he was allowed to manage it as he saw fit, as long as he agreed to serve his lord in war and attend his court when summoned.

Dukes, counts, and viscounts made up a small class of noblemen called barons, who ruled their individual fiefs and owed their loyalty to a superior lord. It was understood, though, that all barons in Charlemagne's empire owed their highest loyalty to the emperor himself. Most knights still did not belong to this nobility. They were elite soldiers, but most were neither landowners nor rulers. The members of the nobility came almost exclusively from a few select families who could trace their ancestry back to Frankish chieftains or Roman aristocrats of the fifth century.

Technically, titles and fiefs were not hereditary. When a vassal died, or failed to fulfill his oath of loyalty, the fief was returned to the lord who had granted it, and he could assign it to another vassal. In reality, passing titles and fiefs on to members of the same family was the most sensible, and therefore the most common, practice.

Charlemagne Demands Highest Loyalty

One of the most persistent controversies of the Middle Ages was whether a vassal owed greater loyalty to his feudal lord or to his king. When Charlemagne was king, he left little doubt, as shown by this general capitulary from Tierney's Sources of Medieval History.

"Charlemagne commanded that every man in his whole kingdom, whether ecclesiastic or layman . . . down to those who were twelve years old, should now promise their fidelity to him as emperor, . . . that all may know this oath contains this meaning:

1. First, that each one voluntarily shall strive, in accordance with his knowledge and ability, to live wholly in the holy service of God. . . .

2. Secondly, that no man, either through perjury or any other fraud, for the flattery or gift of any one, shall refuse to return or dare to conceal a serf of the lord emperor or a district or land or anything that belongs to him. . . .

3. That no one shall presume to rob or do any injury to the churches of God or widows or orphans or pilgrims; for the lord emperor himself, after God and His saints, has declared himself their protector and defender.

4. That no one shall dare to lay waste a fief of the lord emperor or make it his own property.

5. That no one shall neglect a summons to war from the lord emperor; and that no count shall dare to dismiss any of those who owe military service. . . .

6. That no one shall obstruct at all in any way a ban or command of the lord emperor, or to dally with his work or to impede in any way his will or commands. And that no one shall dare to neglect to pay his dues or taxes.

7. That no one, for any reason, shall make a practice in court of defending another unjustly either from any desire of gain or by obstructing a just judgment by his skill in reasoning, or by a desire to oppress another. That every case shall be tried in accordance with justice and the law; and that no one shall have the power to obstruct justice by a gift, reward, or any kind of evil flattery."

It helped to maintain peace between families, and it ensured a continuity of government and of military support.

To keep his loyal vassals content, Charlemagne made certain there was enough land to go around. Most of his kingdom was still uncultivated wilderness, which he could grant to counts, viscounts, or other vassals who were willing to clear the land and farm it. Charlemagne also tripled the size of his kingdom through military conquest. From the territories thus acquired, the king and his vassals could distribute new lands as fiefs, steadily increasing the number of noble families. Charlemagne kept the noblemen busy raising armies and fighting for him, so they had no time to fight against each other.

The Church Obtains Political Power

When the pope crowned Charlemagne emperor of the Holy Roman Empire, he did not bestow any power that Charlemagne did not already have. Still, it was a symbolic gesture that reflected the strong alliance between the emperor and the church. The imperial crown, like God's stamp of approval on Charlemagne's government, gave this government and its capitularies an aura of authority and supremacy over the feudal nobility.

Charlemagne rewarded the church for its support by making it his most powerful ally. He gave nearly two-thirds of the lands

Solid gold and jewel-encrusted, this crown was worn by the Holy Roman emperors after Charlemagne's time. It is now on display in a Vienna museum.

he conquered to the church. Furthermore, he made tithing, or giving a tenth of one's earnings to the church, a legal requirement. In addition, he allowed the church to have its own courts, with complete control over marriages, burials, and wills, three critical areas in matters of inheritance and property rights.

Thus Charlemagne helped to make the church a powerful political and economic institution as well as a religious one. Bishops and abbots controlled large amounts of land. Along with the land came the responsibility to rule and protect the peasants who lived on the land. Therefore the bishops and abbots, needing armies to protect their lands, obtained vassals of their own. In many ways, then, bishops and abbots resembled noblemen more than they resembled other priests. As long as the emperor kept the church's support, the bishops and abbots were powerful allies. In the years following Charlemagne's death, his successors came to rely on that alliance to help check the growing power and independence of the nobility.

2 From Soldiers to Noblemen: The Rise of Knights

No king or emperor has since ruled as much of Europe as Charlemagne did. When he died in 814 at the age of seventy-two, he was buried in his imperial robes beneath the dome of the cathedral in Aachen, his imperial city. Three-and-a-half centuries later, the church he had served so well made him a saint.

Charlemagne's legacy withstood the test of time, but his empire did not. In fact, near the end of his life, he saw emerging threats to it. In the east, warlike Hungarian tribes threatened Bavaria. Raiding Saracen armies from Spain challenged Italy and southern France. Most disturbing of all were the Viking raiders from the north. Through superior seamanship, the Vikings had already conquered many coastal settlements, beginning nearly two centuries of Viking domination of northern Europe.

Vikings sailed from Scandinavia in ships like this to conquer most of northern Europe. They became a growing threat to Charlemagne's empire.

Louis the Pious Inherits Charlemagne's Empire

Before his death in 814, Charlemagne named his son Louis as his successor. Although the tall, handsome Louis resembled his father in many ways, he was not a great warrior like Charlemagne. Raised by priests, Louis was modest, gentle, and gra-

cious; he displayed a lifelong love of learning and a zeal for Christian morals. After Charlemagne's death, Louis expelled his father's former mistresses and his sister's lovers from the court. When his sisters protested, he shipped them off to a convent. His demanding standards earned him the nickname Louis the Pious.

Noblemen Establish Their Own Courts

Many Frankish noblemen began to increase their independence from the emperor shortly after Charlemagne's death. As this decree of approximately A.D. 815, taken from Strayer's Feudalism, *shows, Emperor Louis the Pious, Charlemagne's son, often gave his vassals the right to rule and administer justice on their own land.*

"We grant our faithful man, John, in the county of Narbonne [specific lands] and all the lands he and his men can clear . . . to be held by him and his sons and their heirs without payment or annoyance.

No count, viscount or any of their subordinates, or any public official shall presume to distrain or judge their men who live on their lands, but John and his sons and their heirs shall judge and distrain them. And whatever they judge lawfully, shall be enforced permanently, and if they go beyond the law, they shall make amends according to law. And that this charter shall have full authority, while he and his sons and their heirs shall remain faithful to us and our sons and their heirs, we have ordered it sealed with our ring."

Louis the Pious, Charlemagne's son and heir to the throne.

Louis's chief adviser was a monk, Benedict. Following Benedict's advice, Louis gave the church even more land and power than his father had. During his reign, from 814 to 840, the monasteries continued to grow and prosper, but Louis's own government was beset with troubles. Most of his dukes and counts were busy defending their lands against Viking raiders. Louis did little to help them, and they, in turn, had no more interest in the king's artistic and philosophical renaissance than Louis had in going to war against the Vikings.

A ninth-century Benedictine monk. Emperor Louis relied on the scholarly monks for advice and in return strengthened the monasteries' political power.

The Empire Breaks Apart

As a result, the Holy Roman Empire began to crumble. Few of Charlemagne's former dukes and counts held any allegiance to the government of Louis the Pious. Only the church remained loyal to him. Bishops held courts and administered justice, and monks handled most of the emperor's official business. Most counts and dukes, however, ignored the emperor's decrees and the bishops as well. Many established their own courts of law, calling on their vassals to attend court hearings and judge complaints against their peers.

Although Louis the Pious remained emperor until 840, by the end of his reign he held only a title and no real power. In fact, when Louis tried to bestow part of his kingdom on his youngest son, Charles the Bald, his three oldest sons rebelled, and they gained the support of most of the counts and dukes in the empire. Together, they forced Louis to give up his throne in humiliation.

The Rising Power of Feudal Barons

Then the sons of Louis began to fight amongst themselves for control of the empire, starting an era of feudal conflict in Europe that would last for more than three hundred years. As the empire broke up, confusion reigned among the counts and dukes and their many vassals. For twenty years, the four brothers fought one another. Meanwhile, Viking raiders continued to invade the Frankish kingdom from the north, Hungarian warriors threatened the eastern frontiers of the empire, and Muslims challenged the Franks in the south.

In this violent atmosphere, most landholders were more concerned with keeping their own lands than with defending any of Louis's sons. Most were willing to swear homage to any lord strong enough to help them defend and protect their property. They were far more loyal to the powerful dukes, counts, and viscounts who lived nearby than to any would-be emperor.

The Partition of Verdun Permanently Divides the Empire

None of Louis's four sons could muster enough support from his vassals to control the entire empire. Finally in 843, after one of the brothers had been killed in battle, the three survivors—Lothar, Charles the Bald, and Louis the German—agreed to the Partition of Verdun, dividing the empire into three independent kingdoms. The kingdom granted to Charles the Bald closely resembled modern-day France and Belgium, while Louis the German's kingdom covered most of modern-day Germany and Austria. Lothar retained the title of emperor and reigned over an empire that stretched across the heart of Europe, from northern Germany to central Italy. Realizing that the partition left vassals who lived in one kingdom loyal to lords who lived in another, the three rulers pronounced that all feudal ties between lords and vassals living in different kingdoms were void.

When Emperor Lothar II died without an heir in 869, his empire and the title of emperor were inherited by Louis the German. Thus by the end of the ninth cen-

The three sons of Louis the Pious divided up the Holy Roman Empire among themselves, with Lothar (enthroned) inheriting the title of emperor.

tury, most of Europe was divided into two enormous kingdoms: the Frankish kingdom and the German empire, which was still officially called the Holy Roman Empire. Louis, the German emperor, enjoyed the support of the church. This was vitally important because the church actually had more power and influence than either Louis or Charles, the Frankish king. In fact, it was the church, not the kings and emperors, that provided what little stability remained in Europe following the breakup of Charlemagne's empire.

Bishops and Abbots as Feudal Lords and Vassals

Both Charlemagne and Louis the Pious had given land generously to the church, which, with its enormous landholdings, had become a feudal power. To protect their lands, most bishops and abbots granted large parcels of property to knights as benefices, or fiefs. As a result, many bishops and abbots became powerful feudal barons themselves, capable of mounting vast armies of knights and faithful followers. As time went by, some of the churchmen fell under the influence of more powerful dukes and counts. Others swore their loyalty to the Frankish king or the German emperor, while still others maintained that they were independent feudal lords who owed loyalty to no one except the pope and God Himself.

Charles the Bald Tries to Control the Frankish Counts

This ninth-century capitulary by King Charles the Bald, taken from Frederick Ogg's Source Book of Medieval History, *outlines the counts' duties and rights.*

"We order our counts . . . to give respect to the status of our vassals . . . as they wish to have their own position respected by us. . . .

Let the counts . . . see to it that at no place in their counties shall coins be struck secretly or fraudulently. . . .

Let each count make a list of all the public markets in his county . . . and bring the list to the next meeting of our court, so that we can see what markets are necessary . . . and should be continued . . . and what markets are unnecessary and should be forbidden. . . .

Let the counts . . . and our vassals see that honest measures . . . are made for buying and selling in our towns and villages. . . .

The Franks of each county who have horses shall go to the army under their counts. . . .

Let the counts diligently inquire how many freemen in each county can serve in their army at their own expense. . . .

Let each count list the names of the lords and the names of all immigrants from the regions devastated by the Northmen. . . .

Let our counts know that we are sending our investigators who are to make a special inquiry about how they are obeying the orders which we are now issuing."

The Roman church hierarchy. The pope is at the center, surrounded by bishops and abbots, then priests and members of religious orders, and finally the laity (kneeling in foreground).

This lack of a single focus of loyalty led to serious disagreements over investiture, or the right to assign abbots and bishops. The pope claimed that he alone possessed that right, while both the French king and the German emperor also claimed rights of investiture. In reality, though, it was the powerful counts and dukes who usually selected the bishops and abbots in the counties and duchies.

Since the landholdings of a bishop or abbot were often quite large, and since these officials were lords over many knights, the seats of abbot and bishop became extremely strategic political appointments. Being an abbot or bishop was a way to gain power and wealth. Therefore, counts and dukes often granted abbeys and bishoprics to family members, even if they had no religious training. Many bishops and abbots lived in castles, ruled their peasants and vassals, and fought feudal wars just like counts and dukes.

Inheriting Fiefs and Noble Titles

To help secure economic, military, or political alliances, noblemen not only entered into feudal agreements, they also arranged marriages, assigned bishoprics, and besieged their neighbors' lands. When the son of one nobleman married the daughter of another, a political alliance between the two houses usually resulted. Often the husband in such an alliance benefited by inheriting more than one fief—one from his father and others from father-in-law or uncles. For when a feudal lord died without a male heir, his fief was often passed to a married daughter.

Technically, nothing in the ninth-century fealty oath allowed a vassal's fief or title to be inherited. On the contrary, every lord had the right to reclaim the fief of a deceased vassal. As a practical matter, however, fiefs and titles of nobility were usually passed down from father to oldest son, who usually was the family member best prepared to assume the father's feudal rights and obligations. This heir normally could expect his father's vassals to support him, and he could be counted on to honor his father's feudal oaths.

A medieval royal marriage. In the Middle Ages, marriages were made more for political than for romantic reasons.

Inheriting fiefs was so common by the middle of the ninth century that the practice of primogeniture, or the rights of the firstborn, became custom. Such rights are clearly assumed, for example, in a decree by King Charles the Bald recorded in 877. At that time, Charles was about to leave on an expedition to Italy, so he issued the following instructions in case any of his vassals died while he was gone:

> If a count shall die, whose son is with us, our son [Charles's son, who was left behind to govern in his father's absence] shall choose from among those who were closest to the count a man who will take care of the county . . . until we [Charles] are notified . . . so that we may honor the son . . . with the offices of his father. Our vassals shall be treated the same way. And we expressly order bishops, abbots, counts, and our other *fideles* to make every effort to follow the same rules with their men.[8]

The inheritance of counties and duchies, as well as the titles that accompanied them, had to be approved by the king, but this soon became a formality. Soon people regarded titles as belonging to a particular noble family, or "house." Even when his counts or dukes were disloyal to him, the king had a difficult time replacing them or taking their land from them. In 865, for example, the *Annals of Breton* report that King Charles the Bald had taken several counties away from counts in northern France because they "had done nothing useful to guard the Seine valley against the Northmen (Vikings)"; Charles then gave three of these counties to his most powerful supporter, Robert the Strong, "and with his advice, divided the counties west of the Seine among his [Robert's] supporters."⁹

While Charles did take three counties away from one group of feudal barons, he had needed Robert's backing to do it. In fact, Robert and his vassals probably initiated the action, and Charles had little choice but to go along with it. Charles's declining power over his militant barons can be seen in another account from the same annals two years later. This time, Charles tried to take away the land and title of a count named Gerard while Gerard was away fighting in a feudal war. Charles "took the county of Bourges from Count Gerard in his absence . . . and gave it to Acfrid"; but a year later, Gerard reclaimed his county and his title:

> The men of Count Gerard made war on Acfrid . . . and set fire to a house in which he had taken refuge. When Acfrid was driven out, they cut off his head and threw his body in the fire. Then Charles attacked the County of Bourges and did more evil than can be told. However, he not only failed to avenge himself on Gerard and his counts, but he could not even drive them out of the county.¹⁰

Inheriting a Fief

In 877, this capitulary of Charles the Bald, taken from Frederick Ogg's Source Book of Medieval History *specified what to do with a fief if the eldest son is away on a military campaign when the lord of the fief dies. References to "us" and "our" are forms of the royal "we" referring to the king.*

"If a count of this kingdom, whose son is with us, shall die, our son with the rest of our faithful shall appoint some one of the nearest relatives of the same count, who, along with the officials of his province and with the bishop in whose diocese the same province is, shall administer that province until announcement is made to us, so that we may honor his son who is with us with his honors. . . .

If, however, he had no son, our son along with the rest of the faithful, shall take charge, who, along with the officials of the same province and with the proper bishop shall make provision for the same province until our order may be made in regard to it. Therefore, let no one be angry if we give the same province to another whom it pleases us, rather than to him who has so far provided for it.

Similarly also shall this be done concerning our vassals. And we will and command that as well the bishops as the abbots and the counts, and any others of our faithful also, shall study to preserve this toward their men."

Feudal Anarchy and the Rising Status of Knights

By the year 900, the Frankish kingdom had become a confusing network of alliances formed through feudal oaths, marriage contracts, and inheritance. Almost every lord in France found himself in the midst of a conflict over land. The only thing that really supported anyone's claim to land was the power to defend it. And noblemen who had that power often found reason to claim their neighbors' lands as well.

Any nobleman who wanted to increase his power, or just hold what he had, needed lots of loyal knights. Since land was still more plentiful than money, many noblemen divided their land into small fiefs and granted them to knights. As more knights acquired fiefs and became vassals, they also acquired more political authority and began to be recognized as members of the ruling class.

The first sign of knights' rising status was their appearance in the courts of the dukes, counts, and viscounts, the great lords. In fact, attendance at his lord's court was one of the responsibilities of a vassal. In the days of Charlemagne, the public courts were presided over by a count or duke, and the vassals who attended were other great noblemen. As fiefs became smaller, however, the lords of these fiefs held their own courts, and they could not expect the great lords to attend. Instead, most of the vassals who attended were ordinary knights.

Knights who attended these courts gained political and judicial experience. As lords of small fiefs, which usually consisted of a single village, these knights began to hold courts of their own to judge petty matters that did not interest their lords. These were usually cases involving complaints of theft or other wrongs committed by one peasant against another. Nevertheless, the

A knight pledges fealty to his lord. By the tenth century, knights had achieved the status of nobility.

knights established their authority over their villages, and they became recognized as members of the nobility.

Although the village lord "held" his land, which consisted of a castle or manor house surrounded by a small village of less than a hundred peasants, he did not really "own" it. Rather, he held the right to use the land and to rule the peasants who lived on it, as long as he fulfilled his obligations to the lord who had granted it to him. Thus he became the lowest link in the chain of feudal authority that rose, through increasingly more powerful lords, counts, and dukes, to the king himself.

This chain of command was usually broken somewhere, at the level of a viscount,

The layout of a typical feudal manor shows the lord's castle and chapel surrounded by his fields and a village.

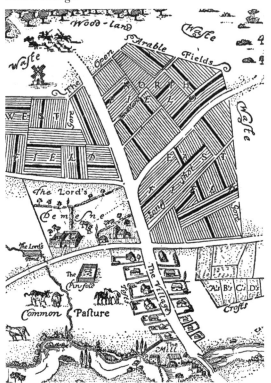

count, or duke, rather than extending all the way to the king in every case. That is, there was no formal legal system, or universally applicable set of laws. Conflicting customs, inheritance claims, feudal obligations, and alliances were a source of almost constant feudal warfare throughout the tenth and eleventh centuries. When such a flammable mixture was touched by the spark of personal greed or dishonesty, it often exploded into private wars between lords.

Of course, any nobleman who accused another of wrongdoing could present his case before the court of a superior lord. Because the presiding lord often decided such cases based on what was most favorable to him, however, the plaintiff was not likely to receive satisfaction. These court hearings probably helped to cause more feudal wars than they prevented.

In fact, most courts recognized trial by combat as a legal way to settle differences. Trial by combat was based on the simplistic belief that God would side with whoever was right. As a result, many lords tried to "prove their rights" by summoning their vassals and leading them to war against rival lords. The stronger the army one could raise, the better his chances of "proving his rights."

The Responsibilities of a Vassal

By the year 1000, the rising stature of most vassals as members of the nobility was reflected in the ceremonial swearing of the feudal oath. This, too, became a widespread tradition during the tenth century. As part of the ceremony, a vassal knelt and

A confusion of laws and customs meant that medieval lords and vassals often fought to determine who owned a particular parcel of land.

placed his hands together between those of his lord. In this position, the vassal swore his loyalty and accepted the conditions of his fiefdom. Then the lord raised the vassal to his feet and "invested" him with his fief.

This part of the ceremony was called the investiture. The lord presented his vassal with a scepter, an ornamental staff symbolizing authority to govern the fief. Next, the vassal usually received a banner that bore his family's coat of arms, which symbolized his nobility. Finally, he was handed a piece of sod, symbolizing the land he was to rule as its new lord.

The feudal oath and the traditional obligations of lords and vassals had become fairly standard throughout most of France and Germany. A letter written in 1020, from Bishop Fulbert of Chartres to Duke William of Aquitaine outlined the duties of the vassal:

> The vassal must promise never to attack his lord, in word or deed, or attack his lord's castle. He should never seduce his lord's wife, his lord's daughter, daughter-in-law, or sister. He must warn of any plots against his lord that he might hear of. He must help his lord in his just wars, and at the very least defend him in his unjust ones. Above all, he must not forsake his lord on the battlefield. If need be, he should find him a horse, even to the extent of giving him his own. If his lord is captured in battle, he must ransom him from his captors. Furthermore, the vassal must take the lord's political and judicial interests to heart. He must advise him, sit on his court, and help him to administer justice, notably in judging his peers.[11]

The Independence of Village Lords

In the two centuries after Charlemagne's death, knights had risen from the status of elite soldiers to members of the nobility. Most of them ruled single villages, and they had considerable autonomy. They interpreted and enforced laws in their villages; they provided systems of justice and defense; and they taxed the peasants as much as they wanted to.

Each village was self-sufficient. The villagers farmed the land, produced grains for food and ale, and raised geese. Craftsmen in each village built the wagons and tools the villagers needed. Millers ground their grain into flour, and bakers baked it into bread.

The lord not only enforced the laws, he owned the land the peasants farmed, the blacksmith shops where they bought their tools, the mills where they ground their grain, and the breweries where they brewed it. The forests surrounding the fief were considered to be the lord's forests. He alone had the right to hunt and fish in them. Any peasant caught poaching—that is, hunting, fishing, or cutting down a tree—was guilty of stealing the lord's property.

Historians estimate that peasants living on feudal estates in Europe made up as much as 80 percent of the total population during the Middle Ages. About half were freemen, who could leave whenever they chose, and the others were serfs, who were legally bound to the fief. As long as the freemen stayed, however, they lived like the other peasants on the fief.

Whether freeman or serf, a peasant was a tenant farmer. He was given a small plot of land to farm, and he paid a share, or tribute, of everything he made from the land—the crops, the milk, the eggs, the fowl, everything—to the lord of the fief.

The peasants were strongly affected by the constant warfare between their lords. As one eleventh-century knight said, "When

This medieval manuscript illumination depicts serfs tending the fields surrounding their lord's castle. If attacked, they took refuge within the castle's walls.

two nobles quarrel, the poor man's thatch goes up in flames."[12] Because of the nearly constant threat of war or raids, most peasants rarely ventured beyond their own villages. Practically every aspect of their lives was governed by their lord. He decided what jobs they were to do and how much food they had to eat. He declared work days and holidays. He could make it nearly impossible for peasants to abandon their village or even to marry outside it. In many ways, the tenth-century lord really was "lord as far as the eye can see."

3 The Norman Triumph: Feudalism in England

In 987 Louis V, the last of Charlemagne's descendants to serve as king of the Franks, died without an adult heir. By this time, the king was little more than a figurehead. Feudal barons had divided most of the Frankish kingdom into seven powerful realms: the duchies of France, Normandy, Burgundy, and Aquitaine, and the counties of Toulouse, Anjou, and Flanders. The dukes and counts who controlled these realms gave their vassals and rear vassals (vassals of counts and dukes) great independence in ruling their fiefs, and that left the king with little power.

The Humble Beginnings of the Capetian Dynasty

In fact, after the death of Louis V, the seven barons elected the next king from amongst themselves. They chose Hugh Capet, a great-grandson of Robert the Strong. Capet was the first in a line of descendants who would rule France for the next eight hundred years. That is why historians often refer to the kings of France as the Capetian dynasty.

The first Capetian kings, however, could hardly be called powerful kings. In fact, as the duke of France, Hugh was the weakest of the seven barons, and it was his relative weakness that appealed to his fellow barons. His duchy was known as the *Ile de France,* a relatively small estate around Paris. It was surrounded by the more powerful duchies of Burgundy and Aquitaine in the south, the county of Flanders in the northeast, and the mighty duchy of Normandy to the north.

Hugh Capet, a descendant of Robert the Strong, was named king of France in 987, beginning an eight-hundred-year dynasty.

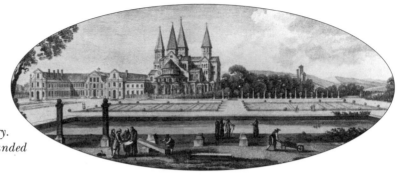

Medieval monasteries were centers of culture and industry. Many famous abbeys were founded in prosperous Normandy.

The Duchy of Normandy Is Founded

Normandy, the land of the Normans (or "Norsemen"), was governed by descendants of Rollo, a great Viking chieftain. In 911, the French king, Charles the Simple, feared that the Vikings might sweep through his entire kingdom. To prevent such an invasion, he offered Rollo an enormous region of northern France if Rollo would agree to become his vassal. Thus Rollo became the first duke of Normandy.

The Normans not only adopted many of the feudal customs of the Franks, they perfected them and built them into a system that made the Norman rulers far more powerful than their lords, the kings of France. So it was that the world's first strong feudal government arose not in France proper, but in Normandy. And the rulers of this feudal government were descendants neither of Germanic warlords nor Roman aristocrats, but of Viking chieftains.

Within a century of the Vikings' acquisition of Normandy, their duchy was the most enterprising and prosperous of the French duchies. Abbey schools and great monasteries sprang up throughout the re-gion. Their armies were unsurpassed. The Normans were accomplished sailors and shipbuilders, too, and with their favorable location they dominated trade routes from England and Scandinavia.

The Powerful Dukes of Normandy

The Norman rulers had another distinct advantage over any other feudal ruler in Europe at the time: they could control their rear vassals. Viking conquerors had thrown out the old Frankish counts and viscounts in northern France and replaced them with loyal followers. They demanded that all the viscounts swear a fealty oath not just to their counts, but first, to the duke himself. As a result, viscounts were obliged to honor the duke first, and their own counts second. Instead of being independent rulers of their own realms, like the viscounts in the rest of France, Norman viscounts were more like government officials, or local ministers of the duke.

Robert I, duke of Normandy from 1028 to 1035, strengthened his control over vassals and rear vassals by taking advantage of

The Duchy of Normandy Founded by Rollo

When Rollo swore his feudal oath to King Charles the Simple in the year 911, the Viking chieftain became the first duke of Normandy. He was hardly the humblest of vassals, however, as we see in this eyewitness account taken from R. Allen Brown's The Normans.

"At the agreed time Charles and Rollo came together at the place that had been decided on. . . . Looking at Rollo, the invader of France, the Franks said to one another, 'This duke who has fought such battles against the warriors of this realm is a man of great power and great courage and prowess and good counsel and of great energy too.' Then, persuaded by the words of the Franks, Rollo put his hands between the hands of the king, a thing which his father and grandfather and great-grandfather had never done; and so the king gave his daughter Gisela in marriage to the duke and conferred on him the agreed lands from the River Epte to the sea as his property in hereditary right, together with all Brittany from which he could live. . . .

The bishops [in attendance] said, 'Anyone who receives such a gift ought to be eager to kiss the king's foot.' [Rollo] replied, 'I have never bent my knees at anyone's knees, nor will I kiss anyone's foot.' But, urged by the entreaties of the Franks, he commanded one of his warriors to kiss the foot of the king. The warrior promptly seized the king's foot, carried it to his mouth and kissed it standing up, while the king was thrown flat on his back. At that there was a great outburst of laughter and great excitement among the people. Nevertheless King Charles, Duke Robert, the counts and nobles, the bishops and abbots swore by the Catholic faith and by their lives, limbs, and the honor of the whole kingdom to the noble Rollo that he should hold and possess the land described above and pass it on to his heirs."

the church's Truce of God. Enacted in 1027, the Truce of God forbade warfare between nobles except on certain days of the year. On all other days, a general truce was observed. By enforcing the truce if someone was fighting on the wrong day of the year or otherwise violating its rules, Robert found good reasons to interfere in the local conflicts among his vassals and rear vassals, ensuring that none of them accumulated enough land or power to threaten him.

The Truce of God

The church's Truce of God was declared in 1027. As described here by Drogo, the bishop of Terouanne in 1063, and recorded by Frederick Ogg in A Source Book of Medieval History, *the truce included ten specific restrictions on feudal war.*

"Dearest brothers in the Lord, these are the conditions which you must observe during the time of the peace, which is commonly called the truce of God, and which begins with sunset on Wednesday and lasts until sunrise on Monday.

1. During those four days and five nights, no man or woman shall assault, wound, or slay another, or attack, seize, or destroy a castle, burg, or villa. . . .

2. If anyone violates this peace and disobeys these commands of ours, he shall be exiled for thirty years as a penance.

3. . . . he shall make compensation for the injury which he committed. Otherwise he shall be excommunicated by the Lord God and excluded from all Christian fellowship. . . .

4. If any violator of the peace shall fall sick and die before he completes his penance, no Christian shall visit him or move his body from the place where it lay, or receive any of his possessions.

5. . . . If anyone takes from another an animal, a coin, or a garment, during the days of the truce, he shall be excommunicated unless he makes satisfaction. . . .

6. . . . no one shall make a hostile expedition on horseback, except when summoned by the count. . . .

7. All merchants and other men who pass through your territory from other lands shall have peace from you.

8. You shall also keep this peace every day of the week from the beginning of Advent to Epiphany, and from the beginning of Lent to Easter, and from the [Monday before Ascension Day] to Pentecost.

9. We command all priests on feast days and Sundays to pray for all who keep the peace, and to curse all who violate it.

10. If anyone has been accused of violating the peace and denies the charge, he shall take the communion and undergo the ordeal of hot iron. If he is found guilty, he shall do penance within the bishopric for seven years."

Pilgrims make their way to a holy shrine. Pilgrimages were common despite their dangers. Many people were ordered by the clergy to make a pilgrimage as atonement for their sins.

After laying this foundation for a feudal state with a strong central government, Robert, a devout Christian, set out in 1035 on a pilgrimage, or holy journey, to Jerusalem. Such a journey in the eleventh century was filled with danger. So his vassals expressed grave concern for his safety, primarily because they did not think Robert had a legitimate heir.

William I, Duke of Normandy

Robert named as his heir his illegitimate son William, whose mother was the daughter of a poor tanner. From the time of his birth, William and his mother had lived in Robert's castle as part of his family. Robert had loved them both deeply, and now he saw, in his teenage son, the potential for a strong and virtuous leader. Thus he declared to his vassals:

By my faith, I will not leave ye lordless. I have a young bastard who will grow, please God, and of whose good qualities I have great hope. Take him, I pray you, for lord. That he was not born in wedlock matters little to you; he will be none the less able in battle . . . or to render justice. I make him my heir, and I hold him [in command] from this present time of the whole duchy of Normandy.[13]

When Robert did, in fact, die en route to Jerusalem, some of his vassals refused to honor William as their new lord. But William responded swiftly and fiercely. He summoned his loyal vassals to war against the rebels, defeated them, and divided their lands among his faithful vassals.

Another example of William's ferocity can be seen in his attack on the rebellious count of Alençon. Some of Alençon's followers hung hides on the castle wall to taunt William by reminding him of his humble birth. Angered by the insult, William attacked Alençon's castle and took numerous prisoners. He cut off their hands and feet, gouged out their eyes, and catapulted all these body parts into Alençon's courtyard.

It did not take so fearsome a warrior long to gain the loyalty of his father's vassals. For the rest of his long reign, William was feared for his brutality. But he was also admired for his fairness and iron rule.

Duties of a Vassal and His Lord

This letter from Fulbert, bishop of Chartres, to William, duke of Aquitaine, written in 1020, is a famous medieval document that summarizes the accepted understanding of the duties of a vassal at the beginning of the eleventh century. The letter is quoted from Brian Tierney's The Middle Ages, *Volume I:* Sources of Medieval History.

"To William most glorious duke of the Aquitanians. . . .

Asked to write something concerning the form of fealty, I have noted briefly for you on the authority of the books the things which follow. He who swears fealty to his lord ought always to have these six things in memory: what is harmless, safe, honorable, useful, easy, practicable. Harmless, that is to say that he should not be injurious to his lord in his body; safe, that he should not be injurious to him in his secrets or in the defenses through which he is able to be secure; honorable, that he should not be injurious to him in his justice or in other matters to him in his possessions; easy or practicable, that that good which his lord is able to do easily, he make not difficult, nor that which is practicable he make impossible to him.

However, that the faithful vassal should avoid these injuries is proper, but not for this does he deserve his holding; for it is not sufficient to abstain from evil, unless what is good is done also. It remains, therefore, that in the same six things mentioned above he should faithfully counsel and aid his lord, if he wishes to be looked upon as worthy of his benefice [or fief] and to be safe concerning the fealty which he has sworn.

The lord also ought to act toward his faithful vassal reciprocally in all these things. And if he does not do this he will be justly considered guilty of bad faith, just as the former, if he should be detected in the avoidance of or the doing of or the consenting to them, would be [disloyal]."

In fact, William managed to keep the support of his vassals even though he further limited their independence. He accomplished this by giving his rear vassals direct access to his courts. Whenever a rear vassal believed that his lord had wronged him or had not given him a fair hearing, he could appeal to the duke himself. In this way, William established a direct link to his rear vassals. While strengthening their loyalty to him, he restricted the authority of their immediate lords, his vassals. Thereafter, if the vassals' judgments did not accord with the duke's, he could overrule them.

The illegitimate son of the duke of Normandy, William conquered England to earn the surname "The Conqueror."

of land with which to reward his loyal vassals. He had already conquered the duchy of Brittany, and his feudal ties and alliances with other French barons kept him from conquering their lands. So William looked north, to England. There he foresaw not only the solution to his dilemma, but the promise of even greater power.

The Norman Link with England

The houses of the duke of Normandy and the Anglo-Saxon king of England were already linked by a series of political marriages between Norman nobility and the Anglo-Saxon nobility. In 1042 William's young cousin Edward the Confessor became king of England. Although Edward was Anglo-Saxon by birth, he had been brought up in William's court, under William's protection, from the time he was ten years old until he ascended the English throne. Edward spoke French, brought French customs to the royal court, and surrounded himself with French friends and advisers. The English people, most of whom were Anglo-Saxon, looked upon Edward as a foreigner, and they resented his rule.

That is why so many of them idolized Edward's brother-in-law, Harold. He was tall, handsome, strong, gallant, and reckless. He was also Anglo-Saxon, and he spoke English. Edward feared Harold's popularity, and he suspected Harold and his father, Earl Godwin of Wessex, of plotting to overthrow him. Because of his suspicions, which turned out to be unfounded, Edward stripped Harold and Godwin of their fiefs and their family claim to the title of earl.

To keep his vassals from rebelling, William used a combination of fear and reward. He rewarded vassals handsomely when they were loyal by granting them large fiefs and other gifts. And those who were disloyal, he swiftly overthrew. For example, he gave huge fiefs to the church for establishing bishoprics and abbeys. Then he appointed his most loyal vassals as the bishops and abbots over these large jurisdictions. In all his feudal ties, William rewarded his vassals well for their loyalty, but he also insisted on direct control of his rear vassals.

Under William's leadership, Normandy prospered, and William became the most powerful baron in all France. He had just one problem: he was running out

Knights: From Soldiers to Noblemen

In the eleventh century, even low-ranking knights became village lords, but as this charter of Count Baldwin of Flanders, signed in 1038 and quoted in Joseph Strayer's Feudalism *shows, some of these village lords were forbidden by their lords from establishing their own courts.*

"I, Baldwin, by the grace of God count of Flanders . . . acknowledge before all my barons that the abbey of Marchiennes was always free from obligations to an advocate. . . . However, because of the present evil state of the world, it needs an advocate for its defense. That I may be the faithful advocate and defender of the church, the abbot gave me two mills and two ploughlands in the town of Nesle. . . . I, however, have given the mills and the land with the consent of the abbot to Hugh Havet of Aubigny, so that he may be a ready defender of the church in all things. If he fails in this . . . he shall lose the land and the advocacy which he holds of me.

And this is what he receives in the abbey's lordship. He shall have one third of all fines in cases where the church has asked his assistance . . . and has gained something by his justice. . . . In time of war, he shall receive from each plough-team two shillings, from half a team one, and from each laborer three pennies. . . . He shall not give orders to the men of the abbey . . . nor hold courts of his own, nor take money from peasants. He is not permitted to buy lands of the abbey, . . . or give its serfs in fiefs to his knights, nor to extort anything from them by violence. . . .

The mark of Baldwin, the marquis who ordered this document to be made. The mark of Adela, the countess. The mark of Eustace, count of Boulogne. The mark of Roger, count of St. Pol. The marks of Sanswalonis, Freardus, Walter, Berneir, Ogier, Dominicus, knights. This court was held by four knights of the advocate [Hugh Havet]: Udo, Ursio, Garderus, Maimbodo."

That was quite possibly Edward's poorest decision because it turned Harold, a strong and loyal vassal, into an enemy. Harold raised an enormous army to reclaim his family's land, and he plundered the southwest coastline of England, destroying castles, villages, and fields as he marched toward London. When Harold

King Edward dismisses Harold. Edward feared that the popular Harold would usurp his throne.

reached the city, the people went out to greet him as their hero. In fear, most of Edward's Norman vassals fled to Normandy, and Edward's severely weakened army fell to Harold. Harold probably could have taken Edward prisoner and claimed the English throne for himself. Instead, he honored the highest value of feudalism: loyalty to his lord, Edward. He simply demanded that his father's fief and title be restored. At Godwin's death a year later, Harold became earl of Wessex.

William's Claim to the English Crown

The Anglo-Saxons revered Harold, so they rejoiced when Edward, who had no children of his own, named him the successor to this throne shortly before his death in 1066. What they did not know at the time was that William, the duke of Normandy, claimed that Edward, his cousin, had already promised the English throne to him. Furthermore, William had briefly held Harold prisoner after a feudal battle in 1064, and as a condition of his release, Harold apparently promised to recognize William as king of England and to assist him in securing the throne after Edward died. On these grounds then, William claimed that he, not Harold, was the rightful king of England.

Officially, however, William's claims had to be upheld by the English witan, or council of earls. Earls, who were the English equivalent of counts, traditionally elected the English king. Normally, the witan's election was a simple formality endorsing the king's choice, but this time the election of Harold antagonized William and set the stage for a showdown between the Normans ruled by William and the Anglo-Saxons under King Harold.

William raised a huge army, with which he intended to conquer England and its Anglo-Saxon king. He promised land, loot, noble rank, and feudal privileges to any Norman who joined his campaign. In September 1066 he set sail across the English Channel with a fleet of seven hundred ships carrying an army seven thousand strong.

Meanwhile in England, King Harold could not worry about William immediately. First he had to put down an invasion from Norway. Harold defeated the Norwegians, but in the meantime, William's mighty army had landed on England's southern coast, and Norman soldiers were burning and thrashing their way through southern England. Harold rode south to stop William, but his army was far too small to be pitted against William's forces.

This scene from the thousand-year-old Bayeux tapestry depicts the Normans, led by William, sailing to England to engage Harold and the Anglo-Saxons in the Battle of Hastings in 1066. The tapestry has been an invaluable document of medieval history and culture.

The Battle of Hastings

Harold's advisers asked him to wait until he could strengthen his army with reinforcements. Reports of murdering and looting by William's army, however, were more than the impatient Harold could tolerate. On October 14, 1066, he caught up with William's army near the town of Hastings and immediately challenged William to remove his foreign army from English soil. William refused, claiming that the English soil was rightfully his. There ensued one of the most famous military encounters in all of western history: the Battle of Hastings.

The Bayeux Tapestry

Much of what historians know about the Battle of Hastings comes from their interpretations of a thousand-year-old embroidered mural known as the Bayeux tapestry.

With evidence gathered from the tapestry and from historical chronicles, historians have pieced together what happened during that nine-hour battle that changed the course of history. More than seventy yards long, the tapestry contains sixty embroidered scenes depicting the entire story of the Norman invasion and providing the world's most complete visual reference to European armor and weapons of the eleventh century.

The tapestry's woven scenes also reflect the traditional feudal values of the age. Its first scene shows Harold swearing an oath of allegiance to William, which was William's justification for the invasion. The scenes that follow show William making preparations for the campaign and receiving sacred relics from the pope. The fleet of seven hundred vessels is depicted plying the waters of the English Channel. Finally, the tapestry depicts the progression of the violent Battle of Hastings.

Harold's undermanned army had positioned itself at the top of a rise. An army of select foot soldiers, or housecarls, formed the front wall of his defense with their kite-shaped wooden shields. Behind them, mounted on horseback, were the Anglo-Saxon knights of the English realm, or at least as many as Harold could summon on such short notice. On the morning of October 14, William marched his Norman army slowly up the hill toward the Anglo-Saxon army. Finally, he ordered a cavalry charge, which was ferociously repelled by Anglo-Saxon foot soldiers brandishing their battle axes. Then the Anglo-Saxon knights rode out to drive the invaders back, but to their surprise, the Norman army did not retreat.

Instead, it stood its ground, and eventually the Normans' superior numbers began to take their toll on Harold's Anglo-Saxon army. The Anglo-Saxons did not have enough archers to counter the Normans' constant shower of arrows. Slowly, the Normans fought their way back up the hill. And when Harold rode out to exhort his troops to fight harder, he was struck by an enemy arrow. He fell from his horse and was immediately surrounded by Norman soldiers.

The Normans did not try to take the Anglo-Saxon king prisoner. Instead, they slaughtered him. They chopped off his head and dismembered his body, scattering arms, legs, and entrails across the battlefield. Historians have concluded that most of William's soldiers must have been mercenaries, or hired soldiers, eager to gain riches through the spoils of war. That may be why they murdered Harold instead of taking him prisoner, which would have been more in keeping with the tradition of nobleman versus nobleman in feudal warfare. As it was, soon after the death of Harold, the dispirited Anglo-Saxon army surrendered the kingdom of England to William, duke of Normandy.

The Norman Conquest

On Christmas Day in 1066, William I was crowned king of England. From that day forward, he was known as William the Conqueror. Before the Norman conquest, the Anglo-Saxon people in England had been invaded and exploited by Vikings and Danes. With the infusion of Norman influence, the English became a more enterprising, seafaring, dominating people. In fact, no foreign nation has successfully invaded England since 1066.

William claimed all the soil of England as his own. This enabled him to reward his deserving followers with fiefs, but it also gave him a chance to establish a feudal government based on the principle of delegated powers, perhaps the Normans' most significant contribution to the evolution of feudalism. According to this principle, all political power is delegated from a higher to a lower lord. The implementation of such a system led to the establishment of an elaborate hierarchy, which we still associate with the European nobility.

Building a Strong Feudal Monarchy

At the heart of the principle of delegated powers was a belief in the divine right of a king to rule over his entire kingdom. The kingdom was the king's fief, granted to him by God, and all noblemen in the kingdom were faithful vassals under his control. What made this principle easier to implement in England than in France? First, William's conquest of the entire kingdom gave him extraordinary power, which he used to advantage by replacing almost every Anglo-Saxon landholder with a Norman vassal loyal to himself. Second, the Anglo-Saxon kings had enjoyed considerable authority throughout their kingdom, and William saw the advantages of retaining that traditional power.

While English earls had their own vassals, called thanes, they also shared authority in their earldoms with the king, who held royal properties, or shires, throughout the kingdom. The English king kept a royal official, or sheriff, in each of his shires, and each sheriff commanded a small army of knights who helped enforce the king's wishes throughout the kingdom.

For more than a century before the Norman conquest, sheriffs had collected *danegeld*, a sort of income tax for the king, from every freeman in the kingdom. The purpose of the tax was to help the king finance royal armies to defend the kingdom from Viking and Danish raiders. Danegeld made the English king the only European monarch who had a source of income that was not dependent on feudal ties.

After William conquered the Anglo-Saxons, he replaced Anglo-Saxon sheriffs with his own force of Norman sheriffs, who continued to collect danegeld. The mixture of Norman feudalism with the traditions of the Anglo-Saxon monarchy enabled William to build a strong kingdom based on feudal loyalties.

The Domesday Census

One of William's first official acts was to take stock of all he had conquered. He demanded a thorough census of the property of every freeman in England: how much land he held; how many knights he had in his service; how many serfs lived on his land; how many pigs, oxen, and geese he had; and what mills, breweries, inns, wagons, and carts he owned. A description in the *Anglo Saxon Chronicle* captures the amazing thoroughness of this eleventh-century census: "[William] ruled over England, and searched it out so with his cunning, that there was not a hide of land in England that he didn't know who had it, or what it was worth, and afterward he put it down in his writing."[14]

One of William's reasons for conducting his census was to establish a basis for replacing Anglo-Saxon noblemen with loyal Normans. As a result, most members of the Anglo-Saxon nobility lost almost everything they owned—their castles, their land, and even their belongings. With few exceptions, the entire Anglo-Saxon population was forced into poverty and serfdom. Not surprisingly, the Anglo-Saxons resented everything Norman—the language, the Norman nobles and officials William had brought from Normandy to administer his government, and especially the census. Anglo-Saxons staged riots and revolts against their Norman conquerors throughout the kingdom, but William's sheriffs punished the Anglo-Saxon offenders brutally, often with death. If their cases were heard in court, the hearings were so swift and their punishments so sudden that the English people likened them to Judgment Day, or, in the contemporary term, "Domesday" (doomsday). To this day, the record of William's census, finished in 1085, is known as the *Domesday Book*.

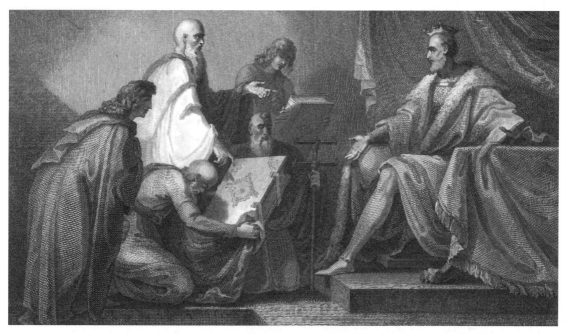

William the Conqueror, sitting on the English throne, receives the Domesday Book, *the census of all Anglo-Saxon subjects and their properties. The book acquired its ominous name from the swift and brutal judgment William's sheriffs meted out to any English subject who resisted the census.*

The Fate of the Anglo-Saxons

After stripping practically every Anglo-Saxon landholder of his lands and titles, William divided England into new earldoms, which he granted to his most important Norman vassals. As with his census, William acted swiftly and brutally. While he inspired admiration from his Norman followers, he reaped only hatred from most Anglo-Saxons. The author of the eleventh-century *Anglo Saxon Chronicle* describes William as a merciless and paranoid ruler who threw his own brother in prison because he suspected him of being disloyal:

> He was a very severe man and violent, so that no one dared to do anything

against his will. He put earls in chains, bishops he removed from their bishoprics and abbots from their abbeys, thanes he put in prison, and finally he did not even spare his own brother, named Odo. Odo was a very powerful bishop in Normandy. . . , and he was the most prominent man next to the king. When the king was in Normandy, then Odo was master in this country, and yet he put him in prison.[15]

While William's conquest ruined many Anglo-Saxons' lives, it presented a golden opportunity for Norman noblemen and freemen seeking advancement. By 1087, just two decades after the conquest, about 200,000 Norman and French settlers had taken root in England. They dominated the nobility, the church, the government administration, and the military. As the Norman king and lords settled in their new kingdom, they introduced the Norman style of feudalism to England, which placed great political power, military might, and wealth in the hands of the king.

For more than a century after the conquest, a few deposed Anglo-Saxon noblemen formed rebel bands. They attacked Norman rulers and tried in vain to reclaim their lands. According to legend, one of these bands, which stole from the rich Norman landholders and gave to the poor Anglo-Saxon serfs, was that of Robin Hood and his merry men. The rebels were more a nuisance than a threat, however, to the Norman nobility.

The English Feudal System

When replacing Anglo-Saxon landholders with Norman vassals, William used his *Domesday* records to assign each new earl a specific amount of property within carefully defined boundaries. From this information, he also determined the exact number of knights each earl owed him.

Robin Hood and his merry men, a band of Saxon rebels, have been immortalized in legend down to the present day.

He also kept several shires in each earldom for himself and assigned lesser Norman vassals to be sheriffs and help him police his kingdom.

In shires throughout the kingdom, William built a network of castles, at which he stationed royal knights. These knights helped the sheriffs control crime and put down Anglo-Saxon rebellions. To finance his building projects, William employed the despised danegeld, or general tax, which, according to the Anglo-Saxon chronicler, made him extremely unpopular:

> He had castles built and distressed poor men greatly. The king was very severe and took from his subjects many marks of gold and more hundred pounds of silver. This he took from his countrymen by weight, with great injustice, and for little need. He had fallen into covetousness, and he loved greed completely. . . . Powerful men lamented it and poor men complained of it. But he was so hard that he did not care for all their enmity. But they had to follow the king's will completely if they wished to live or to hold land or possessions or even his favor. Alas, that any man should grow so proud as to exalt himself, and account himself over all men! May Almighty God show mercy to his soul and grant him forgiveness of his sins![16]

With sheriffs and their knights stationed throughout the country, William controlled crime and made England a safer, more secure land. He also encouraged his earls to build their own castles and man them with knights. In a short time, a vast network of castles had sprung up, making Norman noblemen safe from either an Anglo-Saxon revolt or a foreign invasion. Even the Anglo-Saxon chronicler admitted that William had made England safe and relatively free of crime:

> Among other things one should not forget the good peace which he made in this land, so that a man who was of any account could go across his kingdom unmolested with his bosom full of gold; and no man dared to kill another man, even though the other had done ever so much harm to him.[17]

A typical earl under King William owed his monarch the service of a few hundred knights. The only way he could provide these knights was to grant fiefs to lesser noblemen, each of whom subinfeudated his fiefs among several knights. Some of these knights further subinfeudated their fiefs, creating a hierarchy of vassals and rear vassals much as in France.

Unlike France, however, where feudalism had emerged slowly over several centuries, England adopted a fully developed feudal system from Normandy and combined it with the Anglo-Saxon tradition of a strong king. To be strong, a feudal king had to control his vassals, and the secret to that was controlling the rear vassals.

Therefore, William decreed that every freeman, no matter what his feudal position, must swear allegiance to the king. Furthermore, he required all his rear vassals to swear homage to the king as their liege, or principal lord. In theory, at least, an English vassal's feudal oath to his lord was secondary to his oath to the king. Any vassal or rear vassal who bore arms against the king broke his oath and was branded a traitor. By contrast, if a great lord in France waged war against the French king, a vassal who chose to fight for the great lord was merely fulfilling his feudal obligation.

William ordered castles like this built throughout England for his knights. Their presence prevented any Saxon rebellion.

William also consolidated judicial power throughout the kingdom. He declared murder, rape, arson, treason, and certain other crimes to be "crimes against the kingdom" that could be tried by only the king himself or by his sheriffs. Although earls kept their own courts, they were restricted to cases involving feudal claims or petty complaints.

During the reign of William the Conqueror, England became the home of Europe's most thoroughly organized feudal government. It was built on the principles of feudalism, but it also established a system of delegated political and judicial powers. Of course, the new English barons were not accustomed to such rigid control. Many of them envied the barons of Normandy and France, who had far greater control over the French king. For the next two centuries, the English barons struggled to obtain more power from their king, while on the continent, French kings continued their struggle to gain control over their barons.

4 The Church as Feudal Lord

By 1100, William the Conqueror had introduced the principle of delegated powers to England and had established himself as the one who delegated power. But in France a king was still the puppet of his barons, and in Germany a battle for power was brewing between the "Holy Roman Emperor" and the Roman church.

Pope Gregory Takes on the Kings

The battle over investiture, or the right to appoint bishops and abbots, had been raging in Germany ever since the breakup of Charlemagne's empire in the ninth century. When Gregory VII became pope in 1073, he set out to reform the church, many of whose leaders were unordained priests, bishops, and abbots with stronger loyalties to their noble families and feudal lords than to the church. Gregory attacked the corruption and misuse of church titles and lands by declaring that all bishops and abbots had to be ordained, celibate priests. Furthermore, he declared that any appointment of a church official by a nobleman had to be approved by the pope.

Gregory maintained that the pope's authority was higher than that of any king.

As God's direct vassal, the pope also had the right and duty to confirm or reject men's choice of rulers, including their kings. In an impassioned letter to a German bishop, Gregory claimed that "kings and princes" who rule without the authorization of the church, were "ignorant of God, and covering themselves with pride, violence, and . . . nearly every crime . . . claimed to rule over their peers in blind

In the eleventh century, Pope Gregory VII instituted church reforms and rejected the practice of lay investiture.

lust and intolerable arrogance."[18] Gregory decried the political division, chaos, and constant feudal wars in Europe, and he called for a "European Christian empire," in which kings and powerful barons knelt before the pope as their feudal lord.

Emperor Henry IV

In 1076, the German emperor, Henry IV, denounced these reforms and claimed that he alone had the right to approve or disapprove investitures within his kingdom. Henry even claimed that as Holy Roman Emperor, which was his official title, he had the right to approve the election of the pope. This so angered Pope Gregory that he excommunicated, or banished Henry from the church, stripped him of the title of Holy Roman Emperor, and declared that all Henry's vassals were absolved of any feudal obligations to him.

A large number of German princes and dukes supported the pope in his conflict with Henry because they wanted to curb Henry's power over them. Therefore, they formed a council to officially approve the pope's excommunication of Henry. They defied their feudal oaths to Henry and named their own emperor, Rudolf of Swabia, in his place.

In response, Henry mounted an army comprised of loyal vassals and rear vassals and attacked the noblemen loyal to Rudolf. For four years civil war engulfed most of Germany. Finally in 1080, Henry's army defeated Rudolf and then marched all the way to Rome to throw Gregory out of the papal palace. Henry seized the Vatican, and Gregory was forced to flee. Henry then convened a synod of bishops who excommunicated Gregory and consecrated a new pope, Clement III.

A year later, Gregory died, seemingly defeated by Henry IV. Nevertheless, this pope's uncompromising war against corruption had greatly weakened the nobility's control over the church. While the church gained the loyalty of clergy and flock alike, France and Germany were torn by feudal strife. It was an ideal time for the church to assert itself as the true leader of a unified Christian empire, as Gregory had envisioned. Indeed, just ten years after his death, nobles from Italy to England bowed down to the new pope as their feudal lord.

An Appeal from the Byzantine Emperor

It was Pope Urban II who set Gregory's vision in motion with his call in 1095 to the first great Crusade to drive the Muslims from Jerusalem and restore the Holy Sepulcher, or tomb of Jesus, to Christian rule. This cause united noblemen from France, Germany, and England behind the pope. Several years earlier, the Byzantine emperor Alexius had begun issuing a series of appeals to the Roman pope, asking for his aid in recapturing lands of the Byzantine Empire that had been lost to the Muslims. Alexius promised rich rewards in land and booty for knights who helped drive out the Muslims.

Pope Urban saw a golden opportunity to reunite East and West, or at least to strengthen the ties between them. He realized that such a rapprochement might benefit the West because the Byzantine Empire, with its prosperous middle class composed of merchants, craftsmen, doctors, and scholars,

Who's Deposing Whom?

The ecclesiastical reforms of Pope Gregory VII did not please the German emperor Henry IV, who was unwilling to give up his right to name bishops and abbots. By issuing the following papal edict, found in Brian Tierney's The Middle Ages, *Volume I:* Sources of Medieval History, *Pope Gregory not only excommunicated Henry, he declared that Henry was no longer emperor.*

". . . Oh St. Peter, chief of the apostles, . . . to me as thy representative and by thy favor, has the power been granted by God of binding and loosing in Heaven and on earth. On the strength of this belief therefore, for the honor and security of thy church, in the name of Almighty God, Father, Son, and Holy Ghost, I withdraw, through thy power and authority, from Henry the king, son of Henry the emperor, who has risen against thy church with unheard of insolence, the rule over the whole kingdom of the Germans and over Italy. And I absolve all Christians from the bonds of the oath which they have made or shall make to him; and I forbid any one to serve him as king. For it is fitting that he who strives to lessen the honor of thy church should himself lose the honor which belongs to him. And since he has scorned to obey as a Christian, and has not returned to God whom he had deserted, . . . spurning my commands which, as thou dost bear witness, I issued to him for his own salvation; separating himself from thy church and striving to rend it, I bind him in thy stead with the chain of the anathema [excommunication]. And, leaning on thee, I so bind him that the people may know and have proof that thou art Peter, and above thy rock the Son of the living God hath built His church, and the gates of Hell shall not prevail against it."

was more advanced than the West in architecture, philosophy, medicine, and trade.

Pope Urban also saw an opportunity to restore the glory of the Roman church by reuniting it with the Byzantine, or Greek Orthodox, church. Finally, he realized that if kings and noblemen joined together in this great Christian cause, they would have to stop fighting among themselves. In fact, one reason for the feudal wars in Europe was a shortage of new lands, and a massive campaign through eastern Europe, the Byzantine Empire, and Palestine could yield thousands of new fiefs. Ambitious noblemen could establish entirely new kingdoms in these lands. With promises of new wealth, power, and glory in the eyes of God, the church had something to offer that no king or feudal baron could match.

Pope Urban II Proclaims a Crusade

So it was that in November 1095, at the Council of Clermont in south central France, Pope Urban II made one of the most powerful and persuasive speeches in all history, to one of the most receptive audiences ever assembled. Exaggerating both the atrocities and the successes of the Muslim Turks, he painted a horrifying picture of Jerusalem being overrun by bloodthirsty heathens:

> An accursed race, wholly alienated from God, has violently invaded the lands of [Jerusalem] and has depopulated them by pillage and fire. They have led away a part of the captives into their own country, and a part they have killed by cruel tortures. They destroy the altars, after having defiled them with their uncleanliness.[19]

Having thus aroused the listeners' indignation at the "ungodly" Turks, Urban inspired his audience of Frenchmen with a flattering account of their own glorious and heroic past:

> Upon you, above all others, God has conferred remarkable glory in arms, great bravery, and strength to humble ... those who resist you. Let the deeds of your ancestors encourage you—the glory and grandeur of Charlemagne and your other monarchs. Let the Holy Sepulcher of Our Lord and Savior, now held by unclean nations, arouse you.[20]

Urban next turned the attention of his spellbound audience to more practical considerations. A holy crusade could pro-

Pope Urban II promotes the First Crusade at the Council of Clermont in 1095. The Crusade united European Christians and significantly increased the church's power.

vide land to the conquerors and end quarreling at home:

> For this land which you now inhabit, shut in on all sides by the sea and the mountain peaks, is too narrow for your large population; it scarcely furnishes food enough for its cultivators. Hence it is that you murder and devour one another, that you wage wars, and that many among you perish in civil strife.
>
> Let hatred, therefore, depart from among you; let your quarrels end. Enter upon the road to the Holy Sepulcher; wrest that land from a wicked race, and subject it to yourselves. Jerusalem is a land fruitful above all others, a paradise of delights. That royal city, situated at the center of the earth, implores you to come to her aid.[21]

Urban had given Frenchmen both moral and practical grounds for the Crusade, and he had assured them of their moral and military superiority. He had enticed them with

A preacher stirs the Christian Crusaders to fight to regain the Holy Land from the Muslims. The Crusades sowed the seeds of cultural change in Europe.

the promise of worldly wealth. Only one lure remained—the promise of eternal happiness, and this, too, Urban guaranteed to anyone willing to take up arms: "Undertake this journey eagerly for the remission of your sins, and be assured of the reward of imperishable glory in the Kingdom of Heaven."[22]

Through the crowd a chant began to spread, quietly at first, then louder and louder until practically all the listeners were shouting at the top of their lungs, "Dieu li volt! Dieu li volt! (God wills it)." People by the thousands, rich and poor, nobleman and serf, swore their allegiance to the pope on the spot. "At once," says William of Malmesbury, "some of the nobility, falling down at the knees of the pope, consecrated themselves and their property to the service of God."[23]

For the next nine months, Urban traveled to other cities in France, preaching the Crusade. He assumed the right to absolve vassals from their fealty oaths for the duration of the Crusade, and he guaranteed that the church would protect their fiefs until they returned. Serfs were permitted to leave the soil to which they had been bound so they could join the Crusade. Villagers were freed from the tributes and taxes they owed to their lords, debtors were absolved of their debts, and criminals pardoned for their crimes. Death sentences were commuted to life service in Palestine. The pope assumed the power to do all this, and he was not opposed.

The First Crusade

By the time Urban finally returned to Rome in July 1096, thousands of Europeans, mostly French, were eagerly preparing for the holy war. Only a minority were knights or trained soldiers. The majority were serfs weary of hopeless poverty, younger sons of noblemen eager to carve out fiefs for themselves in the East, merchants desiring to find new markets and new goods, and scoundrels, vagrants, and outlaws. All took up arms in the name of the Cross. One army of twelve thousand, led by Peter the Hermit, a French monk, had only eight knights. This motley, ill-equipped, undisciplined peasant army was known as the Peasants' Crusade.

To be sure, gallant knights and devout believers also enlisted for the sole purpose of restoring the Holy Sepulcher; but for each one of these, hundreds of others joined the Crusade in hopes of finding fortune, and they were determined to have it by whatever means. By diverse routes, these Crusaders made their way to the Holy Land.

A crowd of Crusaders sets sail from Europe for Palestine to wrest control of Jerusalem and the tomb of Jesus from the Muslims. Though some went for religious reasons, most were seeking their worldly fortunes.

When the Crusaders reached Constantinople in the winter of 1096, the Byzantine emperor Alexius was astounded and deeply concerned. He had asked for military aid, but he had not expected to see every knight and foot soldier in Europe camped outside his city! He was not sure whether to welcome this massive force of thirty thousand soldiers as rescuers or to fear them as enemies.

Therefore, along with provisions, military supplies, and horses for the Crusaders, he offered their leaders handsome bribes. In return, he demanded that the nobles swear homage to him and promise that any lands they conquered would be held in fealty to him. Softened by the bribes, the nobles swore their homage.

During the march through Asia Minor, the greatest foes the Crusaders faced were thirst, hunger, and exhaustion. Few reliable maps of the region were available, and most of the Crusaders were not expecting such a long journey. Being accustomed to a land crossed by many rivers and streams, few had brought canteens to store water. They were poorly prepared for the cold winters and even worse prepared for the scorching deserts. Most of them ran out of provisions. Some of the horses died of hunger; others became lame and were killed and butchered for food. Many of the Crusaders themselves died of hunger and disease. Thousands more grew discouraged and abandoned the cause.

The private ambitions of their leaders also distracted the Crusaders. In 1099, for example, Bohemund, a Norman prince, led an army of Crusaders to conquer Antioch, the ancient eastern Mediterranean port city. He established a feudal principality there, making him prince of Antioch. In the same year, another French nobleman,

Now a museum piece, this sculpture of a Crusader and his wife originally adorned their tomb in twelfth-century France.

Baldwin of Bouillon, declared himself Count of Edessa after conquering that Middle-Eastern city. The foundations of great stone castles built by Crusaders to defend their

An engraving depicts the victorious Crusaders holding high the severed heads of the vanquished Turks from whom they captured the ancient city of Antioch in 1098.

conquered lands can still be seen today throughout the Middle East. Formally, the Christian noblemen held these lands in fealty to Alexius. They ruled them, however, as independent estates, establishing Western manors in the Arabian deserts and submitting many of the natives to serfdom.

The Conquest of Jerusalem

In 1099, almost three years after leaving France, the Crusaders reached Jerusalem. The army that had once exceeded thirty thousand had dwindled to about twelve thousand. Owing to the quirks of history, however, Jerusalem was vulnerable when the Crusaders arrived. Ironically, the Turks

they had come to expel had already been defeated by Egyptian Muslims who had made Jerusalem an open city, free to Muslim and Christian worshipers alike. The Muslims' caliph, or chief ruler, offered a truce to the Crusaders.

The Crusaders had not traveled so long and far, however, to be denied their prize. Led by Baldwin and his brother Godfrey, they besieged Jerusalem, and the caliph's army of a thousand soldiers could not resist for long. On June 8, 1099, the Crusaders triumphantly entered the Holy City.

What happened next defies belief. The Crusaders began a mass slaughter of local Muslims, most of them innocent families whose only "sin" was being non-Christian. Raymond of Agiles, a chronicler who witnessed the horror firsthand, describes the

The Crusaders Capture Jerusalem

Fulcher of Chartres was at the Council of Clermont in 1095, and there he swore his fealty to the pope. He accompanied the Crusaders to the Holy Land and recorded this account of the bloody and merciless capture of Jerusalem in 1099 in his Chronicle of the First Crusade, *which can be found in Brian Tierney's* The Middle Ages, *Volume I:* Sources of Medieval History.

"The Franks entered the city magnificently at the noonday hour on Friday, the day of the week when Christ redeemed the whole world on the cross. With trumpets sounding and with everything in an uproar, exclaiming: 'Help, God!' they vigorously pushed into the city, and straightway raised the banner on the top of the wall. All the heathen, completely terrified, changed their boldness to swift flight through the narrow streets of the quarters. The more quickly they fled, the more quickly were they put to flight.

Count Raymond and his men, who were bravely assailing the city in another section, did not perceive this until they saw the Saracens jumping from the top of the wall. Seeing this, they joyfully ran to the city as quickly as they could, and helped the others pursue and kill the wicked enemy.

Then some, both Arabs and Ethiopians, fled into the Tower of David; others shut themselves in the Temple of the Lord and of Solomon, where in the halls a very great attack was made on them. Nowhere was there a place where the Saracens could escape the swordsmen.

On the top of Solomon's Temple, to which they had climbed in fleeing, many were shot to death with arrows and cast down headlong from the roof. Within this Temple about ten thousand were beheaded. If you had been there, your feet would have been stained up to the ankles with the blood of the slain. What more shall I tell? Not one of them was allowed to live. They did not spare the women and children."

The Crusaders lay siege to Jerusalem.

massacre as if it had been the greatest glory in the history of Christianity:

> Some of our men cut off the heads of their enemies; others shot them with arrows, so that they fell from the towers; others tortured them longer by casting them into the flames. Piles of heads, hands, and feet were to be seen in the streets of the city. It was necessary to pick one's way over the bodies.
>
> But these were small matters compared to what happened at the temple of Solomon. . . . What happened there? If I tell the truth, it will exceed your powers of belief. So let it suffice to say this much at least, that in the temple and portico of Solomon, men rode in blood up to their knees and bridle reins. Indeed, it was a just and splendid judgment of God, that this place should be filled with the blood of the unbelievers, when it had suffered so long from their blasphemies.[24]

Bernard of Clairvaux, a reformist monk and a famous champion of the Crusades, now known as St. Bernard, later justified the slaughter: "The Christian who slays the unbeliever in the Holy war is sure of his reward; more sure if he himself is slain. The Christian glories in the death of the pagan, because Christ is thereby glorified."[25]

The victorious Christians immediately established the new kingdom of Jerusalem, which covered most of Palestine. Godfrey of Bouillon took the title of prince of Jerusalem. When he died a year later (in 1100), his brother Baldwin took the loftier title of king. Baldwin divided the kingdom into counties, which his vassals further divided into fiefs. They built their Western-style castles and attempted to establish a

While his soldiers loot Muslim corpses, Godfrey of Bouillon pays homage to the tomb of Jesus after defeating the Muslims who held Jerusalem.

feudal system like the one they had known in Europe.

Unfortunately, conquering Jerusalem turned out to be the easy part; holding on to it was more difficult. The Christian conquest of Palestine became a mockery of the original ideals of the Crusade. Most Crusaders did not stay in the Holy Land for long. Many who had come seeking their fortune in the "land of milk and honey" were bitterly disappointed by what they found there—a dry, infertile wasteland.

The Last Crusades: A Vision Distorted

By 1150, Jerusalem, Antioch, Edessa, and all the other lands conquered by the Christians in the First Crusade had fallen back into the hands of the Muslims. Still, the mystique of the Holy Land and the influence of the church were strong enough to lure knights and peasants alike on three more Crusades to the Holy Land between 1146 and 1204. Despite these efforts, Christians were unable to recapture Jerusalem or any of the other lands in the Near East for long.

The Fourth Crusade to the Holy Land (1202–1204), the last major expedition, exemplifies what a fiasco the Crusades had become. Before the First Crusade in 1096, the Byzantine emperor Alexius had appealed to the West for help. In 1202, a descendant of this emperor, Alexius IV, made his own appeal to the West. Alexius IV claimed that his brother, Alexius III, was a tyrannical ruler who deserved to be overthrown. With a substantial bribe, Alexius IV convinced a group of French barons and Venetian merchants to help him overthrow his brother. If they were successful, he promised to pay them 200,000 marks of silver, equip them with an army of 10,000 men for a crusade to Palestine, and submit the Greek Orthodox church to the rule of the pope in Rome. Pope Innocent III forbade the Crusaders from attacking Constantinople outright. Nevertheless, he gave the Crusaders his blessing for trying to unite the Greek and Roman churches.

The Fall of Constantinople

On June 24, 1203, the Crusaders arrived at Constantinople. None of them had ever seen a city of such splendor, a jewel that reflected the supremacy of the Byzantine civilization, which had developed without interruption since the fourth century. Villehardouin, a chronicler and French Crusader, described the amazement of his fellow expeditionaries when they first laid eyes on Byzantium:

> You may be assured that those who had never seen Constantinople opened wide eyes now; for they could not believe that so rich a city could be in the whole world, when they saw her lofty walls and her stately towers wherewith she was encompassed, and these stately palaces and lofty churches, so many in number as no man might believe who had not seen them, and the length and breadth of this town which was sovereign over all others.[26]

At the sight of so great a force outside their city walls, most of the knights and barons of Alexius III fled the city. The citizens of Constantinople gave Alexius IV and his comrades in arms a heroic welcome—until they discovered what Alexius had promised his Western allies. Indeed, Alexius had bargained away nearly all the city's wealth, forfeited its seven-hundred-year-old religious independence, committed troops to an unpopular campaign to Palestine, and offered to share the city with a group of foreign aristocrats.

The people of Constantinople tried to rebel against Alexius IV and his Western supporters. For almost nine centuries, their fortresslike walls had turned back all invaders. Now, however, the Crusaders had already marched through open gates to a heroes' welcome, and so the city, in turmoil over its own rulers, fell in 1204.

What the Crusaders had marveled at a few months earlier, they now ransacked. They set churches, libraries, and palaces on fire. Untold thousands of masterpieces of art and literature, preserved from the days of the ancient Greeks, were destroyed. Byzantine women were raped; citizens loyal to the opposition were tortured and executed. When he heard about the sack of Constantinople, Pope Innocent III was horrified. He denounced the Crusade and excommunicated its leaders.

The Crusaders abandoned their plan to march to Palestine. They were content to transform the Byzantine capital and its surrounding region into the Latin Kingdom of Constantinople. This they divided into feudal estates, each ruled by a Western nobleman. However, few of the people of Constantinople were willing to become subservient vassals and serfs. As in Jerusalem, the Europeans found it impossible to impose their feudal system on a foreign land that had its own strong traditions. Unable to find enough labor for their agriculture, most of the Latin noblemen eventually abandoned their fiefs and

returned to Europe. Unfortunately, the damage they had done to Constantinople could not be undone. After 1204, the Byzantine Empire never recovered its power or its prosperity.

The idea of a Crusade had once been a powerful tool to raise money and enlist soldiers in an idealistic cause. The First Crusade had put the pope squarely at the top of the feudal pyramid. But power and money corrupt, and the church had once again become extremely powerful, extremely wealthy, and extremely corrupt. Popes such as Gregory VII and Urban II had fought for ecclesiastical reform, but their successors created a monster—an institution that taxed people at will, condemned them to eternal damnation if they resisted, and deposed disapproving noblemen. The Crusades had become just another form of feudal warfare, and an excuse for invading someone else's land.

5 Feudalism and the Rise of Commerce

Although the Crusades failed to fulfill the dream of Pope Gregory VII of a united Christian empire, these holy wars brought dramatic changes to Europe. Before the Crusades began in 1096, the old Frankish kingdom had been divided into just about as many fiefs as possible. Fragmentation had been carried to the limit, and the French king had little power to consolidate his vassals and rear vassals into a unified government. Consequently, no system of government in France extended beyond the boundaries of a single duchy or county.

The French economy was a simple agricultural economy, and most feudal villages were independent, self-sufficient estates controlled by village lords—knights who ruled their fiefs as they saw fit. They declared wars on one another and fought over land almost constantly, but few of these lords had the kind of government organization needed to mount a major

A feudal battle scene. The feudal system of fiefs ruled by knights and nobles made war an almost constant reality. But it also made the battles relatively small and locally contained.

military campaign. In general, the feudal system was best suited for forming small armies based on strong personal loyalties linking lords and vassals.

The main advantage of feudal armies was that they spread the cost of warfare evenly. The knights who made up a feudal army supplied their own armor, horses, and weapons. This made warfare affordable, and the reward of acquiring land as a result of military service made it worthwhile.

It was the promise of land that had attracted Crusaders to form the largest feudal armies of all time. In four major Crusades spread over a century and a half, the great lords of Europe founded feudal kingdoms in Armenia, Edessa, Antioch, Jerusalem, Tripoli, and Constantinople. They divided these kingdoms into duchies and counties, which were subdivided into fiefs, just like the kingdoms of Europe. Soon, however, most European noblemen abandoned their fiefs in the Near East.

Crusaders Bring Back New Ideas and New Tastes

Ignoring the fealty oaths they had sworn that allowed the noblemen to acquire the fiefs, the Crusaders returned to their castles and estates in Europe, bringing with them new ideas and new tastes acquired from their travels. Silks, sugar, and such spices as pepper, ginger, cloves, and cinnamon had been rare luxuries before the Crusades. Now knights and noblemen demanded more and more of these goods. At the same time, the conquest of Constantinople, the transport of pilgrims and Crusaders to Palestine, and shipments of clothes, weapons, and other supplies had

Minters stamp slugs of metal into coins. Money became an important commodity with the rise of trade.

greatly increased trade and travel between Europe and the Middle East. New markets in the Middle East raised the demand for English wool, Italian and Flemish fabrics, and German steel. The growth in trade led to rapid growth and greater prosperity for the European middle class, made up mostly of bankers, merchants, and craftsmen. Better banking techniques and new forms of credit were also introduced from Byzantium. As a result of the Crusades, more goods, more money, more people, and more ideas circulated throughout the West.

The Rise of Chivalry

The new commercialism led to the period known as the High Middle Ages (1150–1350), a time of unprecedented prosperity and enlightenment for most members of

A Medieval Tournament

Among the nobility in the High Middle Ages, tournaments were the most popular of all forms of entertainment. In England, William the Marshal was a frequent tournament champion. But as the following passage from The Life of William the Marshal, *by Robert Fossier, clearly demonstrates, a knight attending a tournament had to be prepared for more than mock battles.*

"William and his companions came to the castle of Joigny . . . [where] they dismounted and waited, fully armed, for their adversaries. Then the countess of Joigny came forth . . . with her ladies and damsels, elegantly dressed, and as beautiful as they could be. . . . The knights . . . were delighted by the arrival of the ladies . . . and one of them said: 'Let us dance while we wait and we won't be so bored.' They took each other's hands and then another knight asked: 'Who will be kind enough to sing for us?' William . . . then began to sing . . . which pleased everyone there. . . .

When he had finished his song . . . a minstrel, who had just been made a herald-of-arms, sang a new song . . . of which the refrain was: 'Marshal, please give me a good horse.' When the Marshal heard this . . . he left the dance without a word . . . and a squire brought him his horse. . . . The other party of knights was approaching, . . . the Marshal rode at one of them, confident of his prowess, and with his strong and powerful lance knocked his opponent off his horse. . . . Then he had the minstrel mount it . . . and the minstrel rode back to those who were still dancing and said: 'See what a good horse the Marshal gave me!' . . . Then, as they saw the other group of knights, they put on their helmets and closed their vizors. . . . Those who had been dancing with the ladies strove with body, heart, and soul to distinguish themselves, and they did so well that everyone was astonished."

the nobility. By 1250, this group included most knights, whose rule over their own villages and courts entitled them to the status of noblemen. This elite class of feudal noblemen and their ladies developed their own unique ideals and customs, which we call *chivalry*. The name comes from *chevallier,* the French word for knight. The ideals of chivalry were personified in the popular romances, or epic poems of the day about legendary knights like Sir Lancelot, one of the knights of the Round Table. Lancelot was a vassal of King Arthur, and the feudal bond between them created a loyalty even stronger than family ties. To women, Lancelot was a guardian; to the poor, he

A manuscript illumination shows Sir Lancelot courting his beloved Guinevere. Lancelot's is just one of a great number of medieval legends about knights and chivalry.

feudal war, the church was also an important supporter of the feudal system. It taught that the feudal hierarchy was part of God's elaborate, unalterable plan, according to which every person was born to a particular station in life. The pope was the direct vassal of God, and all kings and other noblemen were God's rear vassals.

Thus the pope was above all kings, kings were above all dukes, dukes above counts, counts above viscounts, viscounts above simple lords, lords above freemen, and freemen above serfs. This arrangement was thought to constitute God's great design, and anyone aspiring to a higher station than he was born to was considered guilty of sinful pride. The belief in the superiority of the noble class became so entrenched in the minds of men and women that it was not seriously challenged for more than four centuries.

The New Economic Reality

The rapid economic changes that followed the Crusades favored the wealthier and more powerful lords, while many small village lords lost their fiefs—and their status as noblemen. Others clung desperately to their land and their noble titles, although they could barely make ends meet.

A number of these village lords had returned from the Crusades to find their villages nearly abandoned. Although they had left the villages as wards of the church, the church often released the lords' peasants from the bonds of serfdom so that they, too, could join the Crusades. In the last years of the Crusades, many villagers moved to the cities, where employers offered them jobs to meet the growing demands for trade and manufactured goods.

was generous; to the church, he was a servant; and to other knights, he was a brother. Like Lancelot, the knight was expected to be valiant in war, yet he was to treat other knights with honor. Rather than kill a vanquished enemy, he was to take him prisoner and treat him with courtesy, as he would an honored guest.

Although very few knights came close to achieving these ideals, the code itself was nevertheless a clear sign that feudalism had created a civilized society, one in which it was possible even to conceive of such ideals. From the time of the Crusades, the church, despite its flaws and corruption, played a strong role in shaping these ideals. While it officially denounced the brutality and greed often displayed in

The Declining Power of the Village Lords

For the first time, many peasants could choose where they wanted to work, and in growing numbers, they chose the cities. The resulting shortage of labor in the villages forced village lords to compete with one another to attract peasant workers. And for the first time, village lords had to pay wages to their peasants. They also had to give up certain centuries-old rights, such as the right to charge peasants for marriage or burial permissions. All these changes brought new freedom to peasants. They could marry whomever they wished; they could demand wages and even move from village to village—or to the city—in search of the best wages.

Through a careful study of parish records from the thirteenth century, historian Robert Fossier has shown how the migration of peasants affected European villages. Fossier estimates that in 1200 about ninety out of every hundred people living in France and southern Germany were rural peasants, and more than half of those were serfs. By 1300 only about seventy out of a hundred lived in rural villages, and most of them were free. Serfdom had almost entirely died out.

To obtain cash for the peasants' wages, village lords had to transform their farms from self-sufficient units that just met the needs of the villagers to profit-producing enterprises. They had to sell crops and other products for money. With the profits, they bought clothing, boots, dishes, silverware, tools, and other goods made by craftsmen in nearby cities.

A woodcut depicts a medieval city street crowded with the shops of local merchants.

Great Lords Consolidate Their Wealth and Power

Typically, the lowest ranking lords who held the smallest fiefs could not raise enough money to compete with the wealthier, more powerful lords. Many of the former had to break their feudal oaths, forfeit their fiefs to their lords, and become mercenary soldiers, hiring themselves out for cash to fight for any lord who was willing to pay them.

A tax collector collects tolls from people using a bridge. Collecting tolls for passing over bridges or through private property became a common practice in the Middle Ages.

Most land lost by the small village lords fell into the hands of the wealthier nobles, especially counts and dukes. These great lords managed to take advantage of the new commercialism in many ways, such as charging tolls to travelers who crossed their lands. Merchants and bankers in the thirteenth century transported large quantities of merchandise and money from city to city. The highways they traveled still passed through wild territory, where the threat of robbery was ever present. Large and small landholders alike demanded tolls from the travelers in return for protection while crossing their land, but the great lords took in the most money from these tolls because they held the most land, especially surrounding the large cities.

In addition, many cities began to hold huge semiannual trade fairs, attended by merchants from all over Europe. The cities needed to assure fair trading practices and to protect both citizens and visitors from thieves. Since law enforcement and justice were still in the hands of nobility, most cities signed charters with viscounts, counts, or dukes who agreed to provide protection, law enforcement, and justice in return for tax payments.

The great lords took advantage of their new monetary wealth to increase their power. They turned practically every aspect of the feudal relationship into a financial one. For example, they hired mercenaries instead of relying solely on their vassals to organize armies. The process of subinfeudation had carved fiefs into increasingly smaller parcels, and often as many as four or five levels of feudal lords separated a duke or count from the village lords in his duchy or county. That made summoning an army rather risky, especially since most vassals were obliged to give their lords only a total of forty days' military service per year.

Until the twelfth century, money had been more scarce than land, so giving away land for military service made good sense. By the thirteenth century, these conditions had changed. Vacant land had become scarce, which is one reason the noblemen were dividing it into increasingly smaller pieces. When more money began to circulate after the Crusades, great lords could avoid the confusion and limitations of feudal agreements by hiring soldiers for cash. As great lords depended less on their vassals and more on mercenaries, the traditional loyalty between vassal and lord began to wane. The emphasis on personal loyalty gradually shifted to an emphasis on money.

Feudal Oaths Become Financial Contracts

Most lords interested in organizing a military campaign preferred hiring mercenaries. By the same token, many lords summoned to war by their overlords preferred to hire mercenaries to go in their place. The traditional feudal lord of the tenth, eleventh, and twelfth centuries had been just an amateur statesman but a well-trained knight. He spent most of his youth honing his battle skills and devoted relatively little time to reading, studying, or learning to administer his civic duties. But by the thirteenth century, that, too, was changing. Many lords had become professional statesmen but were amateur soldiers

at best. Although technically most noblemen were still knights, many of them were knights in name only.

As a result, many vassals replaced the original feudal promise of military service with a promise to pay their lords a standard price for hiring mercenaries to fight in their place. In England, this payment from a vassal to his lord became known as *scutage,* or "shield money." The following treatise, written by an official of King Henry II of England shows that Henry preferred scutage payments over traditional feudal service.

Occasionally, when enemies threaten or attack the kingdom, the king orders that a certain sum be paid from each knight's fief, such as one mark or one

---

The Advantage of Hiring Mercenaries

King Henry I preferred hiring mercenary soldiers to relying on his own English vassals. This writ from 1127, taken from Brian Tierney's The Middle Ages, *Volume I:* Sources of Medieval History, *shows how Henry converted the fealty obligations of most of his vassals from military service to scutage payments.*

"Henry, king of the English, his archbishops, bishops, abbots, earls, etc., greeting. Know that to the church of St. Aetheldred of Ely, for the love of God, for the souls of my father and mother, for the redemption of my sins, and on the petition of Hervey, bishop of Ely, I have forgiven 40 pounds of those 100 pounds which the aforesaid church was accustomed to give for scutage whenever scutage was assessed throughout my land of England; so that henceforth forever the church shall on that account give no more than 60 pounds when scutage is levied throughout the land. And so let the aforesaid church be quit in perpetuity of the aforesaid 40 pounds.

Witnesses: Roger, bishop of Salisbury; Geoffrey, my chancellor; Robert, keeper of the seal; . . . [several knights are also named as witnesses]."

A medieval woodcut depicts a tenant of a knight's estate paying the rent on his land.

well, usually in the form of aids and reliefs. Traditionally, aids were payments that vassals made to secure a lord's release from captivity. By the thirteenth century, dukes, counts, and other great lords had developed a list of special occasions for which they demanded aids from their vassals. If a duke hosted a celebration for the knighting of his son, he demanded aids from his vassals. If a daughter was to be married, he demanded aids.

No matter how absurd the reason or outrageous the demand, low-ranking noblemen had little choice but to pay. They could present their complaint in their lord's court, or even in *his* lord's court, but the practice of demanding excessive aids was so widespread that only extreme cases were punished. A vassal who preferred not to complain could organize a rebellion among his fellow vassals or just pass the new cost down to his peasants in the form of additional taxes. The second tactic was the most typical solution.

Another important source of income from the feudal tie was the relief payment that a lord charged a new vassal whenever a fief changed hands. Relief was a customary form of inheritance tax dating back to the earliest days of feudalism, when a fief was only a temporary grant, and a vassal's son had to pay the lord to keep his father's fief. By the twelfth century, the fief was recognized by all feudal courts as hereditary, but most lords continued to charge reliefs anyway. As the great lords began to consolidate their power, many of them demanded outrageously high reliefs from their vassals. They took even greater advantage when a vassal died without an adult male heir. In such instances, the lord often took over the fief or assigned it to another nobleman who managed it as a

pound, to provide wages or bonuses for soldiers. For the king prefers to expose mercenaries rather than his own people to the chances of war. This payment, because it is reckoned according to the number of knights each vassal owed, is called shield-money, or scutage.[27]

Aids, Reliefs, and Marriage Permits

Scutages represented one form of the shift of feudal oaths in the twelfth century from personal commitments to financial ones. The result, once again, was to put more money into the hands of the great lords. Most of these lords took advantage of their financial superiority and demanded other financial concessions from their vassals as

Matchmaking for Cash

During the reign of King Henry I of England in the first half of the twelfth century, noblemen negotiated for strategic marriage arrangements to increase their landholdings. King Henry took great financial advantage of his ancient rights for granting wardships and marriage rights to his vassals and rear vassals. The following records from the king's treasury, cited by Joseph Strayer in Feudalism, *show just how lucrative Henry's wardship and marriage rights were.*

"Alice, countess of Warwick, renders account of 1,000 pounds and 10 palfreys to be allowed to remain a widow as long as she pleases, and not to be forced to marry by the king. And if perchance she should wish to marry, she shall not marry except with the assent and on the grant of the king, where the king shall be satisfied; and to have the custody of her sons whom she has from the earl of Warwick, her late husband.

Hawisa, who was wife of William Fitz Robert, renders account of 130 marks and 4 palfreys that she may have peace from Peter of Borough to whom the king has given permission to marry her; and that she may not be compelled to marry.

Geoffrey de Mandeville owes 20,000 marks to have as his wife Isabella, countess of Gloucester, with all the lands and tenements and fiefs which fall to her.

Thomas de Colville renders an account of 100 marks for having the custody [wardship] of the sons of Roger Torpel and their land until they come of age.

William of St. Mary's church, renders an account of 500 marks for having the custody [wardship] of the heir of Robert Young, son of Robert Fitzharding, with all his inheritance and all its appurtenances and franchises; that is to say with the services of knights and gifts of churches and marriages of women, and to be allowed to marry him to whatever one of his relatives he wishes; and that all his land is to revert to him freely when he comes of age."

A medieval marriage festival. Paying dearly for an advantageous marriage became common in the Middle Ages.

ward until the vassal's son came of age or the daughter married. In the meantime, the lord often kept most of the revenues from the fief for himself.

Since marriages often determined who would inherit a fief, great lords tightened their control over their vassals' marriage plans. When a vassal's oldest daughter was first in line to inherit his fief, the lord took an active role in finding a husband who would suit his political and military interests. If the vassal's family disapproved of the proposed arrangement, the lord charged the vassal for exercising the right to refuse.

The Money Fief

Although financial arrangements replaced military service in many feudal relationships, many knights still provided the traditional military service. Rather than continuing to give away land to these soldierly knights, however, some lords offered them an annual payment of money, which became known as a "money fief." Many great lords found that the money fief made vassals more loyal than the one-time gift of land. Lords who did not receive the service agreed upon could simply withhold the annual payment. That was much easier than forcibly taking a piece of land defended by a fortress. Perhaps the best known example of a money fief was the payment of 500 pounds per year that King Henry I of England granted to Count Robert II of Flanders in 1103.

By offering this money fief, Henry accomplished two things. First, he obtained a huge military commitment—a thousand knights—from Count Robert, and second, he undermined Robert's commitment to

his liege lord, King Philip I of France, who was Henry's most dangerous enemy. The oath sworn by Henry and Count Robert demonstrates what major concessions Henry was able to win from Robert by offering him all that money. Even though Philip was technically Robert's liege lord, this agreement clearly favored Henry:

> If King Philip plans to attack King Henry in England, Count Robert, if he can, will persuade King Philip to stay at home. . . . And if King Philip shall invade England and shall bring Count Robert with him the count shall bring as few men with him as he can do without forfeiting his fief to the king of France.[28]

By 1200, feudalism had become as much an economic system as a political and military one. A money economy had made it possible for the great lords to extend their power and prestige, while the number of people ruled by lesser feudal lords dropped sharply. Money began to replace personal loyalty as the critical element of the feudal oath. By the same token, wealthy noblemen could now offer money, rather than loyalty, in exchange for land.

The Buying and Selling of Feudal Property

As loyalty and military service gave way to financial arrangements, feudalism began to yield to commercialism. It was only a matter of time before the land itself came to be regarded as a private possession that could be bought or sold. Even though the importance of personal loyalty diminished,

A New Wrinkle: The Money Fief

After the Crusades, noblemen often found it simpler and more effective to offer their vassals annual money payments as fiefs instead of land. As evidenced by this writ of King Henry I of England in 1103, the money fief often inspired greater loyalty and service from the vassal, too. This writ is taken from Joseph Strayer's Feudalism.

"Robert count of Flanders pledges to King Henry by faith and oath . . . that he will help him to hold and defend the kingdom of England against all men, . . . saving his fidelity to Philip, king of France. If King Philip plans to attack King Henry in England, Count Robert, if he can, will persuade King Philip to stay at home. . . . And if King Philip shall invade England and shall bring Count Robert with him, the count shall bring as few men with him as he can do without forfeiting his fief to the king of France.

After Count Robert is summoned by the king of England, he shall get a thousand knights together as quickly as possible in his ports, ready to cross to England. And the king shall find . . . enough ships for these knights, each knight having three horses.

And if King Henry wishes Count Robert to help him in Normandy or in Maine . . . the count shall come there with a thousand knights and shall aid King Henry faithfully, as his ally and lord from whom he holds a fief.

And if at this time, King Philip shall attack King Henry in Normandy, Count Robert shall go with King Philip with only twenty knights, and all his other knights shall remain with King Henry.

The king promises to protect Count Robert in life and limb, . . . and to assure him against the loss of all his land . . . as long as the count shall hold to these agreements. And in return for these agreements and this service King Henry will give as a fief to Count Robert 500 pounds of English money every year."

there was another important aspect of feudalism that did not die out so quickly. Possessing land still meant possessing political and judicial power. Thus, when a lord sold his fief, he officially sold as well his judicial and political duties and all feudal ties. All his vassals became vassals of the new owner, and all the peasants living on the fief became subjects of this new lord.

Many wealthy lords, including the king of France, used this scheme throughout the thirteenth century to add to their landholdings and consolidate their power. But buying and selling fiefs was a tricky business that often led to chaos, confusion, and serious conflict. A nobleman who bought a fief could easily find himself with disloyal vassals, and a vassal could suddenly find himself in the fealty of a bitter enemy. Such conflicts often ended up in the courts of the European kings or emperor, and this, too, gave the monarchs an opportunity to extend their influence over the feudal barons. The following decree, made in 1158, shows how the German emperor Frederick I attempted to resolve the numerous conflicts that arose in his kingdom when noblemen bought and sold their fiefs:

> We have heard bitter complaints from the princes of Italy . . . that the fiefs which their vassals hold from them are either used as security for loans or sold without the permission of their lords . . . whereby they lose the service owed, and the honor of the Empire and the strength of our army is diminished.

Having taken the advice of bishops, dukes, margraves, counts . . . and other leading men, we decree, God willing, this permanent law: No one may sell or pledge the whole or part of a fief or alienate it in any way without the consent of his lord from whom he is known to hold the fief.[29]

Multiple Homages

Such restrictions helped resolve many conflicts, but a new source of confusion was rising in the thirteenth century as a result of the commercializing of feudalism: many noblemen began swearing their fealty to several different lords at once. Traditionally, a vassal could have but one lord because the essential part of his oath was personal loyalty and military service, which he could offer to only one lord. When money became the central part of the agreement, however, a nobleman who

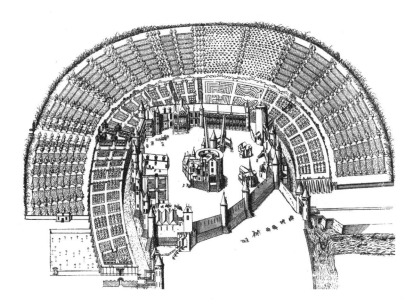

The growth of a money economy allowed wealthy nobles to build great, luxurious estates like this ornately designed French chateau.

wanted to increase his landholdings could acquire fiefs from several different lords at once and satisfy his multiple feudal oaths by paying a scutage to each.

Some attempts were made to preserve a vassal's personal loyalty to his original, or liege, lord. That way, if two of a vassal's lords fought, the vassal's first duty was to his liege lord. Even this principle, though, was soon rendered meaningless by vassals who swore homage to a *first, second,* and sometimes even a *third* liege lord. These multiple homages often produced complex fealty oaths, such as the one that follows, sworn by John of Toul in the early thirteenth century. John had *four* liege lords, and in this oath to the count of Champagne he attempted to sort out his loyalties:

> I, John of Toul, make it known that I am the liege man of Lady Beatrice, countess of Troyes and of her son, my dearest lord count Thibaud of Champagne, against all persons, living or dead, except for the liege homage I have done to lord Enguerran of Coucy, lord John of Arcis, and the count of Grandpré.[30]

Although commercialism diminished the significance of the feudal oath in the thirteenth century, noblemen still held a monopoly on political, military, and judicial power. But the growth of a money economy, the decreasing role of personal loyalty, and the rise in paid military professionals led to an ever-greater concentration of power in the hands of kings and a few great lords. Especially in England and France, men and women learned to identify themselves not as subjects of a feudal lord, but as citizens and subjects of a king.

6 The Decline of Feudal Power and the Rise of Kings

While kings and their most powerful barons wrestled for political control after the Crusades, the church had not lost all its influence. Ecclesiastical, or church-officiated, courts continued to be important, especially for settling marriage, divorce, and inheritance disputes. Also, the demands of a more commercial economy gave the church an important new role to play, that of educator. The rising class of bureaucrats—mostly court clerks and administrators—were almost all educated in monasteries and in universities run by the church. Since they were among the few medieval citizens who could read and write, these church-trained clerks and administrators exerted an influence far beyond their official positions. Kings and great lords relied on them to administer justice, record court proceedings, and keep financial records.

Until the twelfth century, most criminal and civil complaints had been settled by a consensus of vassals meeting in their lord's court. Few written records were kept from these hearings, so local custom and the word of the local lord were the basis of law.

In the ecclesiastical courts, on the other hand, church-trained monks and scholars had continued the traditional Roman practice of recording all judgments. This gave the ecclesiastical courts a

An ecclesiastical court in the Middle Ages. Church courts, unlike civil courts, kept records of proceedings.

record of precedents, or examples of how cases had been decided in the past. It was not long before other lords began to hire these ecclesiastical clerks to administer justice in their courts as well. This practice was especially advantageous to the greater lords because they no longer had to rely strictly on vassals to attend their courts.

The Establishment of Feudal Law

Gradually the clerks compiled their records of court cases into books of feudal law, such as the influential *Libri feudorum*. This book of legal precedents, first compiled by court clerks in northern Italy around 1150, was soon being used in courts throughout Europe. The *Libri feudorum* and other books of feudal law reinforced the principle of delegated powers, which meant in this context that no lord had authority to hold court or pass judgment except through the authority passed down from a superior lord. The French kings of the twelfth and thirteenth centuries took advantage of this principle to begin asserting their rights over powerful feudal barons.

Louis VI and the Rise of the French Monarchy

During the twelfth century, however, the French kings still could not match the military strength of their barons. That is why Louis VI, when he became king of France

Louis VI of France used the new feudal law to boost the comparatively weak authority of the king in France.

in 1108, began to hire mercenary soldiers. Louis VI was a shrewd politician who also gained the support of the bishops and abbots in his royal domain. With their help, he waged ceaseless war against his barons. One baron after another was summoned by Louis VI to appear before his feudal court, charged with various crimes against the crown. More often than not, the barons ignored the summons, whereupon Louis, declaring a breach of the feudal oath, attacked the noblemen's land.

Conquering a powerful baron was not easy. For sixteen years the king fought one powerful baron named Thomas of Marle. Several times he burned Thomas's main castle to the ground, but each time the baron managed to rebuild it. Gradually, though, this fierce lord, who had become the terror of the countryside, lost the support of his vassals and surrendered his fief to the king. Militarily, the king of France was still no match for the king of England, or even the duke of Normandy, but by the time Louis VI died in 1137, the French king was at least the master of his own duchy.

England and Normandy: The Struggle for Power

Louis VI had also replaced many rebellious barons in his duchy with loyal vassals, who paid him handsomely in scutages. These he had used to build a strong military foundation for his son Louis VII, who faced strong opposition from many of his barons when he assumed the throne in 1137. One of the new king's most aggressive rivals was the House of Blois, which controlled the counties of Blois and Champagne and was allied with both Normandy and England. In

King Louis VI and His Battles with Thomas of Marle

When Louis VI assumed the throne of France in 1108, his kingdom was still controlled by independent, strong-willed barons like Thomas of Marle. In a wonderful example of the vivid style of historical writing developed in the Middle Ages, Louis's biographer Suger describes the king's ongoing battle with Thomas, as found in Frederick Ogg's Source Book of Medieval History:

"While King Louis was busy with many wars, Thomas of Marle laid waste the territories of Laon, Rheims, and Amiens, devouring like a raging wolf. He spared not the clergy—fearing not the vengeance of the Church—nor the people for humanity's sake. And the devil aided him. . . . Slaying all men, spoiling all things, he seized two manors, exceeding rich, from the abbey of St. John of Laon. He fortified the two exceeding strong castles, Crecy and Nogent, with a marvelous wall and very high towers, as if they had been his own; and made them like to a den of dragons and a cave of robbers, whence he did waste almost the whole country with fire and pillage; and he had no pity.

The Church of France could no longer bear this great evil; wherefore the clergy . . . proceeded to pass sentence of condemnation upon [him]. . . . And the king was moved by the plaints of this great council and led an army against him right quickly . . . straight against the castle of Crecy. . . . He stormed the strongest tower as if it were the hut of a peasant, and put to confusion the wicked men and piously destroyed the impious. Because they had not pity on other men, he cut them down without mercy. None could behold the castle tower flaming like the fires of hell and not exclaim, 'The whole universe will fight for him against these madmen.'

After he had won this victory, the king, who was ever swift to follow up his advantage, pushed forward toward the other castle, called Nogent . . . and he attacked the wicked castle, broke open the abominable places of confinement, like prisons of hell, and set free the innocent; the guilty he punished with very heavy punishment. . . . Athirst for justice, he ordered that whatever murderous wretches he came upon should be fastened to a stake, and left as common food for the greed of kites, crows, and vultures. And this they deserved who had not feared to raise their hand against the Lord's anointed."

fact, Theobald, the count of Champagne, and his brother, Stephen of Blois, had ambitions of ruling Normandy and England, respectively. Their uncle was Henry I, who was both king of England and duke of Normandy. Since Henry had no sons of his own, Theobald and Stephen claimed that they were next in line to inherit Henry's titles. When Henry died in 1135, Theobald claimed the duchy of Normandy, while Stephen was accepted by the English council of earls as their new king.

But Henry had a daughter, Matilda, one of the most forceful women in the history of the Middle Ages. Matilda, who was married to Geoffrey, the count of Anjou, had no intention of forfeiting her rightful claim to the English throne and the duchy of Normandy. So after Henry died, she and her husband Geoffrey challenged the brothers of Blois and claimed the throne of England and the duchy of Normandy for themselves. Matilda, displaying extraordinary talents in this male-dominated era, led an army to England to challenge her cousin Stephen, while sending Geoffrey against Theobald in Normandy.

Technically, all the contestants for the duchy of Normandy and the throne of England were vassals of Louis VII, the king of France. Louis sided with Geoffrey and Matilda, and with his aid, Geoffrey ousted Theobald from Normandy and named himself the new duke of Normandy.

King Henry II Dominates Both England and France

Louis VII may have believed that he had made his kingdom more secure by helping Geoffrey defeat the House of Blois. In doing so, however, he helped create a new and even stronger threat to the French kingdom in the House of Anjou. When Geoffrey died in 1151, the son of Geoffrey and Matilda, Henry II, became both duke of Normandy and count of Anjou. But Henry was not nearly finished. Just a year later, he became duke of Aquitaine by marrying Eleanor of Aquitaine, who had just been divorced from Louis VII. As a result, Henry controlled three times as much of France as his lord, King Louis VII.

But Henry was still not finished; he had his eye on the English throne, for which his mother, Matilda, was still fighting. Indeed, while in England, Matilda had gained the support of several powerful earls in her campaign against King Stephen. The feudal wars between the supporters of Matilda and Stephen left the kingdom in a state of almost total anarchy for twenty years, until Henry II found a way to end the civil war peacefully. He promised Stephen that he and his mother would stop fighting if Stephen would name Henry as his successor to the throne. Stephen agreed, and when he suddenly died two years later, in 1154, Henry II became king of England as well as the most powerful lord in all of France.

On both sides of the channel, though, Henry had many rebellious vassals. Most of his earls in England had taken advantage of twenty years of civil war to regain their own independence. Both Stephen and Matilda had given away huge fiefs as bribes to secure the support of barons. Now these barons defied the new king by consolidating their power and military strength, building fortresses, and making treaties among themselves. Henry II, however, had the treasuries of three great fiefs in France to work with. This gave him the money to build huge mercenary armies, and with these armies he set to work restoring the supremacy of the English royalty that his great-grandfather, William the Conqueror, had established in England.

Henry II Establishes Common Law— for Everyone but the King

Henry demanded even more feudal rights than William had dared to claim. He claimed the right to approve marriages and to recommend husbands for the heiresses of all his vassals. He demanded aids from any vassal whose son became a knight or whose daughter married. Upon a vassal's death, Henry took possession of the fief in question until the heir had paid the required relief in full. If anyone refused his demands, Henry sent his armies to raid the objector's land and take over his castle or burn it to the ground.

Within a few years, the English king's sheriffs and justices were riding through the kingdom once again, collecting taxes, fining criminals, and filling the royal treasury. Henry II used his court system to further curb the powers of his earls and gain the loyalty of his rear vassals. He declared that specific crimes "belong to the sword of the king." In other words, certain cases could be tried only by the king's sheriffs, not by other noblemen:

These cases belong to the sword of the King: homicide, whether done secretly or openly. Justice in this kind of case belongs to the King alone or to those to whom he or his ancestors gave it. In the same way, cutting off or breaking a

These carvings of Henry II and Eleanor of Aquitaine adorned their royal tomb. Henry was not only the sovereign of England but the most powerful lord in France as well.

man's limbs, . . . robbery, . . . rape, . . . arson, . . .premeditated assault, assault inside a house, assault on a peasant . . . , assault on the King's highway, assault on one going to the King's court, . . . breaking of truces made before the King's judges, and all pleas concerning military service or coinage belong to the King alone.[31]

King Henry II also adopted measures to protect his rear vassals from the oppression of earls and other great English lords. Traditionally, a vassal wronged by one of these great lords had a difficult time obtaining justice in a court made up of his lord's peers. So Henry declared that any rear vassal who believed he had not received justice in the court of his own lord could appeal directly to a royal sheriff.

By such measures, Henry II restored his great-grandfather's claim that the first loyalty of every nobleman in the kingdom was to his king, not to his immediate lord. At the same time, these measures helped fatten the royal treasury. Every plaintiff in a royal court had to buy a writ, or permission, to have his case heard. Henry also made other innovations to the court system to increase his wealth and power.

In a decree known as the Assize of Clarendon, he established the use of grand juries to determine whether evidence existed to charge a person with a crime. Those who were charged and subsequently found guilty had to pay heavy fines to the royal courts. If the accused was hanged, the king confiscated all his property. Likewise, if a suspect managed to flee before he could be brought to court, the king took possession of all his property.

Henry II's legal innovations marked the beginning of English common law: for the first time in English history, all laws throughout the kingdom were subject to appeal in the royal courts. These innovations took away much of the power of the feudal courts. Henry even declared that no lord had the right to take any legal action against a vassal without the king's writ: "It should be known that according to the custom of the kingdom, no one is required to answer in the court of his lord concerning any of his fiefs without the writ of the lord King."[32]

King Henry II of England instituted a new system of law that laid the foundations for English common law.

Henry II Encounters His Strongest Foe

Having stripped his feudal barons of most of their judicial powers, Henry II now sought to do the same to the church. His confrontation with the church, and its highest English official, Thomas Becket, is one of the most poignant stories in Western history.

For the first eight years of Henry's reign, Thomas Becket was the king's right-hand man. Although an ordained priest, Thomas was a brilliant politician who was more interested in political affairs than in religion. Under Henry, he assumed the title of chancellor of the kingdom, and he

King Henry II Revives the English Monarchy

After nearly twenty years of English civil war, from 1135 to 1152, the English king had lost much of his control over his barons. The Chronicle of William of Newburgh, *cited by Brian Tierney in* The Middle Ages, *Volume I:* Sources of Medieval History, *describes how King Henry II went about restoring the landholdings and the authority of the king:*

"The king, considering that the royal revenue was small which had been large under his grandfather, because the crown lands through the weakness of King Stephen had been transferred for the most part to many other lords, ordered these to be resigned completely, by whomsoever held, and to be returned to their former condition. The men who were prominent in the royal towns and manors brought forward charters, which they had either extorted from King Stephen or received from him for service. But since the charters of a usurper ought by no means to harm the right of the legitimate prince, they could not be safe with these documents. And so at first angry, then frightened and saddened, with difficulty indeed, but nevertheless wholly, did they resign these things which had been taken and retained so long as if by legitimate right.

The king therefore carried out all these things in this district according to his wish, and then went to the north of England. Here he found that Hugh de Mortimer, a brave and highborn man, had been rebelliously holding for many years the royal stronghold of Bridgenorth. When he was ordered to be content with his own and to return those things which he possessed by royal gift, he refused most obstinately and prepared to resist in whatever ways he could. But that his pride and indignation were more than his courage appeared in the outcome. For the king quickly collected an army and besieged Bridgenorth, which after a day's siege surrendered; and he pardoned this man, humbled and suppliant, whose heart a few days before had been the heart of a lion."

helped the king enormously in forging the supremacy of the royal government. Thomas enjoyed the king's greatest confidence, and he had nearly as much power and wealth as the king himself.

In 1162, Henry II planned to extend his power over the church by issuing the Constitutions of Clarendon. This document declared the king's authority over the church courts, his right to try priests and clerks of the church in royal courts, and his rights as feudal lord over church lands. Among these feudal rights, Henry claimed the right to take custody of any bishopric or abbey that became vacant, as well as the rights of investiture in the appointments of new bishops or abbots.

To help him persuade the church to accept this subservient role, Henry gave his friend Thomas a new title. In addition to chancellor, Thomas became archbishop of Canterbury, the highest ranking church official in England. But this new title had an effect that Henry had not counted on.

When Thomas became archbishop, he underwent a profound conversion. He gave up his stately palace, his royal clothes, and his noble friends. He even resigned his position as chancellor. He adopted the attire and the humble life of a penitent sinner. And he became the leading defender of church rights, in direct opposition to his friend and benefactor, King Henry II. For two years Thomas blocked the church's approval of the Constitutions of Clarendon, until Henry ordered him arrested. Then Thomas escaped to France, and from there he sent an appeal for help to Pope Alexander III. The pope took Becket's side and threatened Henry with excommunication unless he dropped the charges against Thomas and restored his powers as archbishop of Canterbury.

The Death of Thomas Becket

In 1169, Henry submitted to the pope's demands, and Thomas returned triumphantly to England. As soon as Thomas resumed his position as archbishop, however, he defied Henry again by excommunicat-

A penitent King Henry II begs forgiveness and submits to corporal punishment before the tomb of Thomas Becket, his friend whom he had had killed.

ing all the English bishops who had signed the Constitutions of Clarendon. At the time, Henry was away attending to responsibilities as the duke of Normandy. When he received news of Thomas's action, he exclaimed, out of sheer frustration, "What! Shall a man who has eaten my bread . . . insult the King and all the kingdom, and not one of the lazy servants whom I nourish at my table does me right for such an affront?"[33] Four knights who heard Henry's complaint returned to England, and on December 30, 1170, they killed the archbishop while he was praying at the altar of the cathedral in Canterbury.

The entire Christian world reacted in horror at Thomas's death. The church condemned Henry and declared Thomas a saint. A shrine to Thomas was built in Canterbury, and pilgrims flocked to it by the thousands, claiming that miracles were worked there. Although Henry ruled for nearly two decades after Thomas's death, he was ridden with guilt, and he became a weak, ineffective king. He appealed to the pope for forgiveness, and he rescinded the Constitutions of Clarendon, restoring all the rights and property of the church.

The Downfall of Henry II

Henry's queen, Eleanor of Aquitaine, and his sons became bitter as they watched Henry dismantle the powerful monarchy he had so painstakingly built. Finally, they plotted to overthrow him, and in the unsuccessful attempt, Henry's eldest son was killed. First Henry ordered that Eleanor be imprisoned, then he banished her as a traitor. His two surviving sons, John and Richard, left England on their own accord, traveling to France to plot their father's overthrow with the new French king, Philip II.

Before they could attempt another overthrow, Henry II died. Before his death in 1189, the broken-hearted king went to Canterbury as a penitent pilgrim. The last three miles of the rocky road he walked with bare and bleeding feet. Throwing himself on the ground before the tomb of his one-time companion, Thomas Becket, he begged the monks for their forgiveness.

Although the last half of the reign of Henry II was a testimony to a broken spirit, it did not rub out the important advances of monarchy that were made while he was on the throne. Henry greatly strengthened and unified the government of England. He brought discipline and order to a rebellious nobility, and he limited its power. And even though he gave back to the church the judicial powers and feudal rights he had taken from them, in the years that followed, the royal courts reclaimed and increased their jurisdiction, limiting and gradually eliminating both the feudal and ecclesiastical courts. Henry II had established the principle of common law and the political supremacy of the king over the feudal barons and the church in England.

Philip II Breaks the English Stranglehold on France

At the time of his death in 1189, Henry II was far more powerful than the king of France, Philip II. As duke of Normandy and Aquitaine and count of Anjou, Henry had been officially Philip's vassal, but along with other powerful French barons, Henry had offered a serious threat to the French king. However, Philip II was the kind of ruler who seized every opportunity, legitimate or otherwise, to increase his power. He used every possible means, including war, the buying and selling of feudal alliances, and the arranging of strategic marriages, to increase the territory of the royal domain. Philip was pragmatic, shrewd, courageous, and, perhaps most important, ruthless. He also possessed the patience to exploit the mistakes of his enemies.

Philip devoted most of his reign to breaking the English king's grip on France. He started by stirring up Henry II's sons against him. In 1173, 1183, and 1189, he supported feudal revolts against their father.

King Philip II of France. Philip was cunning and ruthless in his bid to steal power from the English kings.

The French king consistently prodded and rewarded Richard's vassals for rising up against their absent lord, and upon his return from the Crusades in 1193, Richard had to go directly to France to put down these rebellions. Although he defeated his French vassals in battle, Richard never regained their loyalty. Richard devoted the remainder of his reign—and huge portions of the English royal treasury—to his feudal wars in France. The effect of these wars on England was disastrous.

To finance his military expeditions— first the Crusade and then the campaigns in France—Richard demanded excessive aids from his English vassals and oppressive taxes from their subjects. At first, his reputation as the courageous leader of the Crusades helped him win the confidence of his English subjects. But when he left the rule of England in the hands of his sheriffs and drained the royal treasury so that he could hold onto his lands in France, barons turned against him. After all, they wondered, how did it benefit them to pay for his adventures in France?

Though none of the revolts succeeded, Philip forged an alliance with Richard I, Henry's eldest son. When Richard succeeded Henry as the English king in 1189, Philip took advantage of this alliance.

The Reign of King Richard the Lion Heart

In 1190, Philip persuaded Richard to join him in leading the Third Crusade. Shortly after the rulers reached Palestine, however, Philip returned to France, leaving Richard to lead the Crusade alone. While Richard was carving a place for himself in history through his battles with the Muslim sultan Saladin, Philip was busy carving up Richard's lands in France.

Throughout his turbulent reign, Richard managed to keep both his kingdom and his fiefs in France. But in 1199, while besieging the castle of one of his French vassals, he was killed, and his brother John succeeded him to the throne.

King John: The Wrong Man for the Wrong Time

John's vassals in France were rebelling and waging war against him. His English barons were trying to force him to withdraw from France. And the royal treasury was nearly drained. It was a crucial moment, a time that called for a strong yet diplomatic king. King John was neither.

In fact, he probably could not have turned more vassals against him if he had tried. One of his first major mistakes was marrying the fiancée of one of his most important French vassals, the count of Poitou. To make matters worse, the marriage arrangement he disrupted would have formed an alliance between two of his most powerful French vassals, the count of LaMarche and the count of Angoulême. Both houses now revolted against John, and they appealed for justice to King Philip, who was technically John's feudal lord. Charged with stealing his vassal's fiancée, John was summoned to appear before Philip's court. When he refused to appear, Philip declared that John had betrayed his feudal oath and deprived John of all the fiefs he held in France.

The abusive reign of England's King John inspired his barons to later draft and force him to sign the Magna Carta.

Of course, such a declaration meant little. It gave Philip a legal reason for driving John from France, but John still had far greater resources than Philip. Nevertheless, Philip continued to chip away at the seemingly invincible armor of his English rival. And once again, King John played right into his hand.

When Philip declared that King John's fiefs in France had been forfeited to the French crown, he gained one important ally: Arthur, count of Anjou and duke of Brittany, who also happened to be King John's nephew. By traditional feudal customs, Arthur's first loyalty should have been to John, who was his liege lord. But Arthur broke that tradition by dissolving his fealty to his liege lord and swearing homage to Philip, his king. English kings and Norman dukes had been commanding this kind of loyalty from their rear vassals for a hundred years, but this was one of the first times a French king had done so. As a result, many of Arthur's own vassals in Brittany and Anjou followed him to war against King John.

In the summer of 1203, John captured Arthur and imprisoned him in one of his French castles. Arthur was never seen alive again, and John was blamed for his murder. Enraged by this barbaric, unknightly act, more of John's French vassals rebuked him and switched their allegiance to King Philip.

In a span of three years, King John lost Anjou, Brittany, and the county of Poitou to the French crown. With this remarkable good fortune, King Philip next set his sights on Normandy. In England, King John had no luck persuading his barons to help him defend Normandy, and so it, too, fell to King Philip.

The Battle of Bouvines

John was not about to give up his French holdings without a fight, however. So he raised a huge war chest in England through the usual means: taxation and a call for aids. At the same time, he sent large sums of money to Germany to buy the support of the German emperor, Otto of Brunswick, and several German princes. In addition, John succeeded in forming an alliance with two of Philip's vassals, the counts of Flanders and Boulogne.

John persuaded these new allies that King Philip was hungry for power and would go on taking lands until he was stopped. Together they made a plan to stop him: John was to attack Paris with a huge army from the south while Otto, the counts of Flanders and Boulogne, and the German princes marched against Paris from the north.

If John had not created so many enemies for himself in France, the plan might have succeeded, and John might have regained all he had lost. Instead, he met strong resistance marching north toward Paris, especially from the barons in the counties of Poitou and Anjou. As a result, John's northward march was delayed, and his German and French allies marched against Philip alone from the north.

The End of English Domination in France

Philip made a smart response. Ignoring John's armies in the south, he gathered the largest army he could and met the allied forces from the north at a place called Bouvines. His great victory at the Battle of Bouvines in 1214 sealed his place in French history. He became known by his subjects as Philip Augustus. The Battle of Bouvines also sealed the fate of the German emperor Otto, who was forced by his barons to step down in favor of his challenger, Frederick II. For all practical purposes, this also marked the end of English domination in France. Of all the French lands the English had held at the beginning of King John's reign, only Aquitaine remained loyal to him, and its barons were too independent to be strong allies.

The outcome of this great battle weakened the monarchies in Germany and England and strengthened their feudal barons. In France, it had just the opposite effect. The counts of Flanders and Boulogne were forced to swear their allegiance to the French crown. The realm of Philip Augustus now included Normandy, Brittany, and Anjou, greatly increasing the wealth and the military might of the French monarchy.

King Philip II's victory over the English at Bouvines in 1214 earned him the surname Augustus.

Bailiffs Take Control of Local Government

Near the end of the twelfth century, bailiffs (or "baillis") had considerable power to control local village lords, but they remained under the control of the king or lord who hired them, as shown in the following ordinance, issued by King Philip Augustus in 1190. This translation comes from Strayer's Feudalism.

"First, we order our *baillis* to establish in each of our towns four prudent, law-abiding, and respectable men; no business of the town shall be transacted without the advice of at least two of them. . . .

And we establish *baillis* in each of our lands, who shall fix a day called an assize each month in their bailliages. On this day all those who have complaints shall receive justice without delay, and we shall have our rights and justice. . . .

Moreover, we order that our dearest mother, the queen, and our beloved and faithful uncle, William archbishop of Reims, shall hold a court at Paris every four months to hear the complaints of the men of our realm and to decide them for the glory of God and the welfare of the realm.

We also order that at these meetings . . . our *baillis* shall come before them and tell them of the affairs of our land.

If any of our *baillis* shall do wrong . . . we order the archbishop and the queen . . . to send us letters, telling which *bailli* has done wrong and what he did. . . . Then we, with the aid of God, shall punish them in such a way . . . that others may have good reason to be deterred."

In a little over a century, the struggle among the monarchs, the barons, and the prelates of Europe had dramatically changed the functioning of three major institutions: the monarchy, the nobility, and the church. Although its influence was still felt in every aspect of medieval society, the church's possession of land and its direct role in government had declined. So had the role of village lords, who came under the control of the great lords. In England and Germany, where monarchs of the twelfth century had ruled their barons with an iron fist, setbacks in foreign affairs now weakened their base of power at home. In France, by contrast, where the barons clearly had held the upper hand before 1200, King Philip II had tripled his royal domain and obtained military supremacy over his nobles. As the twelfth century gave way to the thirteenth, kings and feudal barons throughout Europe stood at a crossroads, squaring off against each other over political, judicial, and military authority.

Chapter

7 The Final Days of Feudalism

King Philip Augustus had established a strong foundation for the French monarchy. He had driven the English out and solidified his hold over the most powerful duchies and counties in France. Of the six great barons who once controlled the French kings, only the duke of Brittany remained independent, but he did not have the military might to threaten the king. The other great fiefs—Normandy, Burgundy, Anjou, Aquitaine, and Flanders—had all been divided into a number of smaller fiefs held by members of the House of Capet.

A Royal Government Emerges in France

In the century following the death of Philip Augustus in 1223, his successors—Louis VIII, Louis IX (St. Louis), Philip III, and Philip IV—put together all the necessary pieces for a strong royal government. One piece of the puzzle was the judicial system. Like the English kings, the French kings began to use their royal courts to control the great lords. Any vassal who believed that his case had not been decided fairly in his lord's court could now appeal directly to the king. This opened all the

great fiefs to the king's judges and officials.

One such case, heard in the court of King Louis VIII in the year 1224, demonstrates just how far the king's powers had advanced. Jean de Néelle, a vassal to the countess of Flanders, appealed to the royal court because he felt he had not received justice in the countess's court. When King Louis VIII ordered the countess to address Jean's complaints before the royal court, she refused. The following excerpt from a clerk's report shows how the countess was overruled by the royal court:

> Since there had been a dispute between the Countess of Flanders, and Jean de Néelle, Jean appealed to the king's court against the countess for failure to do justice. The countess claimed that Jean de Néelle . . . ought to be judged in her court and that she was ready to do justice in her court through Jean's peers. Jean de Néelle, on the other hand, said that he refused to go back to the countess's court under any conditions, because she had failed to do him justice and because he had appealed to the king's court about this failure. It was judged that the countess must answer him in the king's court.[34]

This could not have happened in France a hundred years earlier, when the

King Louis IX of France exemplified the ideal king: just, pious, and merciful. His exemplary life was recognized by the church in 1297 when he was declared a saint.

French nobility controlled their own courts and ruled their lands independently. By the thirteenth century, royal law had a strong influence in most of the duchies and counties of France. Between 1226 and 1270, King Louis IX (St. Louis) extended royal powers even further by controlling private warfare among his nobles. He enacted numerous laws that complicated and frustrated any efforts to seize another nobleman's land. He decreed that before attacking your neighbor, you had to give him notice, and you had to ask his relatives whether they wanted to be included in the war. If your enemy asked for a truce, you had to grant it. And you could not slaughter your enemy's peasants or burn his crops. St. Louis's royal officials traveled throughout the land to enforce these laws against private warfare.

Lay Administrators Take Over Local Government

Many of Louis's royal officials were professional administrators and judges educated by the church. Unlike clerks and administrators of the twelfth century, however, they were not clergymen or church officials. By this time, the church had established universities in Paris and other major cities where a growing number of young men from noble families went to study law and philosophy.

A medieval class at Oxford University in England. By the thirteenth century, universities in Europe were educating laymen as well as clergy.

Noblemen began to hire these lay administrators, just as they had once hired church officials, to help govern their lands. An intelligent, well-educated lay administrator could keep better records than his lord or his lord's ancestors had kept. He could improve accounting methods and the collection of taxes and tributes from the lord's subjects. Soon this new class of civil servants had replaced many lesser vassals in local government, just as mercenaries had taken their place on the battlefield.

In fact, many of the young knights and barons of lower rank became lay administrators employed by great lords. Dukes and counts hired them as bailiffs, or chief administrators, to oversee the administration of justice, taxation, and law enforcement within specific districts of their duchies or counties. As an administrator for a duke or count, the bailiff was paid a good salary, but he had no claim to the land, and he was usually appointed for only a four- or five-year term. Then he had to move on to another district. This lack of tenure prevented the administrators from building any real political power.

The Diminishing Role of Village Lords

By the middle of the thirteenth century, village lords in France had lost most of their political, judicial, and military responsibilities to the great lords and their paid bureaucrats. Most of them held their land and were entitled to some payment of tributes from serfs. But peasants were escaping from serfdom in record numbers, and those who stayed in the villages had to be paid for their labor.

In effect, most local lords were becoming gentlemen farmers. Of course many retained their official titles and even some official obligations to their dukes and counts. In most ways, however, small fiefs had become like private property, and their peasants were essentially employees, free to quit and move on whenever they chose.

Even large fiefs were bought and sold like private property. In fact, a sales document from the year 1239 shows how King Louis IX bought the entire county of

Mâcon. Although not a large county, Mâcon occupied a strategic position on one of the main trade routes to Italy. The count and countess of Mâcon agreed to sell their county to King Louis for a large lump sum plus an annual income:

> I, John, count of Mâcon, and I, Alice, the countess, his wife, give notice to all men now living and yet to come, that we have sold . . . the county of Mâcon to our dearest lord Louis, the illustrious king of France and his heirs. We have sold the county with everything pertaining to it . . . whether in fiefs or in domains . . . retaining no rights or claims. And the lord king, for this sale . . . gives us 10,000 pounds of Tours in cash and a rent of 1,000 pounds a year assigned on lands in Normandy. . . . All this, John the count, and Alice the countess have sworn on holy relics to preserve and observe firmly and inviolably. . . . Done in the year of our Lord 1239 in the month of February.[35]

The French King Establishes Firm Control of His Barons

Louis IX was also the first French king to collect regular taxes from all his free subjects, as the English kings had done since the time of William the Conqueror. In France, the counts and dukes had been powerful enough to prevent the king from taxing their subjects. Consequently, the French kings had relied strictly on feudal obligations, such as aids, reliefs, and scutages. Therefore, Louis IX proposed a compromise to his barons. He offered to split the proceeds of a general tax with them if they would administer the tax for him.

By the time St. Louis's grandson, Philip IV, came to power in 1285, the French monarchy had developed a bureaucracy for administering justice and collecting taxes. Its band of professional bureaucrats and jurors had grown into the Parlement of Paris, essentially the supreme court of the land. Royal tax collectors had developed a financial "chamber of accounts," although royal taxes still required the approval of the great lords.

The Estates General

Traditional feudal obligations remained between the king and his direct vassals, the great lords of France. Besides the great lords, though, Philip had to listen to the citizens of his great cities, which were

King Philip VI of France presides over the Estates General, his advisory council representing the nobility, the church, and the free citizens.

growing in importance and wealth. To balance the interests of all his constituents, Philip formed the Estates General. This council, which was entrusted with the responsibility of approving all royal taxes and royal laws, compromised representatives from the nobility, the clergy, and the free cities.

While the Estates General had the authority to disapprove the king's policy, it could not make policy itself. And since it represented the interests of the nobility, the church, and city tradesmen, it usually helped the king balance his policies against the interests of any single group.

In centuries past, the authority of the French king depended heavily on the approval of his feudal lords and of the church. Now, the barons and the church played the role of advisers, and they shared that role with bureaucrats and wealthy merchants who did not belong to any feudal tradition whatsoever. In fact, the tie between the king and his barons was the last remaining element of the feudal system in France. And at last, the king was clearly the sovereign lord of his barons.

English Barons Challenge King John

Unlike the French king, the king of England had held considerable power over his barons ever since the Norman conquest. King John had squandered some of that power, but he was still considered the most powerful ruler in Europe when he planned his attack on Philip Augustus in 1214. When Philip emerged victorious at the Battle of Bouvines, however, John returned to England to face an almost certain uprising from his barons.

John had taxed his feudal domains to build up an enormous war chest. He had demanded huge relief payments and unreasonable scutages from his vassals, and gambled it all on his campaign in France. If he had won, he would have been the master of Europe, and he could have either crushed his rebellious barons or bought them off. When he lost, the English barons took advantage of his momentary weakness and demanded that he recognize their feudal rights.

The Magna Carta

The year after his defeat at Bouvines, John was presented by his barons with a charter that defined exactly his rights as their feudal lord. The charter fixed the sums the king could charge for reliefs. It laid down rules for placing a fief under the king's wardship when no adult heir was present. And it specified that the king could not levy general taxes without consulting his barons. This charter, which King John was forced to sign on June 15, 1215, was the Magna Carta. Its historical significance stems primarily from its thirty-ninth article:

> No free man shall be taken, or imprisoned, or deprived of his land, or outlawed, or exiled or in any other way destroyed, nor shall [the king] go against him or send against him except by legal judgment of his peers or by the law of the land.[36]

Article 39 clearly states the principle of English common law. Henry I had established this principle that all free men in the kingdom should live under one common code of justice. As legislators, enforcers,

The Magna Carta, a Final Pitch for Feudal Power

King John's barons took advantage of his weakness after his losses in France and forced him to sign the Magna Carta. The two "charters" of the Magna Carta cited here are taken from Frederick Ogg's Source Book of Medieval History. *Although historians often refer to the Magna Carta as the foundation of English common law, its original purposes were to limit the powers of the king and to preserve some of the rights of the feudal barons.*

"Charter 12. No scutage or aid shall be imposed on our kingdom except by the common counsel of the realm, except to ransom [the king's] body, make [the king's] eldest son a knight, or marry [the king's] eldest daughter. . . .

Charter 14. And to secure the common counsel of the realm for imposing an aid, except in the three aforesaid cases . . . [the king] will summon archbishops, bishops, abbots, earls and greater barons by . . . sealed letters, and . . . will also summon by . . . sheriffs . . . all those who hold directly from [the king] . . . and in all the letters the reason of the summons shall be expressly stated . . . and the business shall proceed on the day assigned by the summons according to the advice of those present, even if all those summoned do not come."

A dismayed King John is forced by his barons to sign the Magna Carta, limiting the king's powers and establishing English common law.

and final judges of common law, however, the English kings often had placed themselves above that law. The thirty-ninth article of the Magna Carta was meant to make the king subject to the same laws as everyone else. The king could not take any action against a free man without judgment by the proper court. This is the origin of the concept of "due process of law."

At the time the Magna Carta was drafted, however, its main purpose was to restrict the power of the English king and to restore some of the power of the feudal barons. For a brief time, it did both. In fact, during the reign of John's son, Henry III, the barons controlled the royal government. They did not allow the king's sheriffs to enter their lands, and they took possession of the sheriffs' courts.

The Changing Military Role of the Medieval Knight

The domination by the English barons was short-lived, though, for they had little military power. Just as in France, the lower levels of the nobility were no longer composed of loyal knights who responded to their lord's call to arms. A new kind of military technology was developing in Europe, and King Edward I, who succeeded his father Henry III in 1272, was among the first to take advantage of it. This new military relied on the archer, who did not have to be a knight. While Edward still depended on a few loyal knights to lead his armies, he manned them with commoners from the countryside, who were trained to handle the longbow and the crossbow. Steel-tipped arrows shot from these powerful

new weapons could pierce even the strongest armor. Edward and his faithful knights worked out tactics for using knights and bowmen together. They changed the makeup of the army from a collection of elite knights reinforced by mercenary bowmen to a body of infantry and archers led by a few knights. These tactics gave the English armies a superiority that they maintained for several centuries, but they also brought an end to the era when knights were the most formidable soldiers on the battlefield. Off the battlefield, dependence on knights to manage local governments continued to decline as well.

England's King Edward I revamped his army to emphasize the role of archers rather than of knights. Such an army was stronger and did not rely on the loyalty of the nobility.

In the thirteenth century, archers replaced knights as the primary military force in medieval armies.

Putting an End to Feudal Oaths

Edward I restored most of the royal authority his father had forfeited to the English barons, and he took steps to further diminish the feudal system in England. His most effective measure was to halt the practice of subinfeudation, or dividing a fief into ever smaller fiefs. For four centuries, this practice had created chains of fealty that sometimes placed six or seven lords between the actual landholder and the king. Edward decreed that any feudal landholder who divided, sold, or granted any part of his fief to another gave up all future claims to that land, including the ac-

ceptance of a feudal oath. In other words, existing fealty oaths were to be honored and could be inherited, but no new ones could be created. Edward also declared that no more land could be given to the church or any other organized "corporation."

Edward I Establishes a Parliament

Edward's strategy of undermining the structure of feudalism and preventing the church from obtaining more land put even more power into the hands of the great barons and the royal government. His formation of that government parallels the emergence of the royal government in France. In 1295 Edward formed what has become known as the Model Parliament. It

A medieval drawing depicts King Edward's Parliament, formed in 1295. Like the French body, it represented royalty, nobility, clergy, and free citizens.

was comprised of two knights from each shire, two city leaders from each free city, and representatives of the clergy. "What touches all," Edward declared, "must be approved by all."[37] Before long, the parliament was recognized as the only body with the authority to approve royal laws. This was the origin of the English Parliament.

By 1300, the conditions that had given rise to feudalism in France and England had disappeared. The relationship of lord and vassal was no longer important as a means of either raising an army or providing local government. The common law of an entire kingdom was replacing the feudal laws and customs of a village or group of villages. Public servants, authorized by a king and his counselors, took the place of knights, who once held political power as a private possession. The practice of feudalism was giving way to the modern state.

Lingering Influences of Feudalism

These changes did not occur overnight, however, and many of the influences of feudalism continued to shape European governmental, military, and social institutions until the twentieth century. Creating national governments and a class of civil servants was a slow process of trial and error. While philosophical arguments over absolute monarchy versus democracy swirled through the universities and the courts of Europe, the emerging governments were a patchwork of feudalist elements, trade associations, and royal governments. In fact, the monarchy in Germany actually became weaker in the fourteenth century, and Germany remained a loose coalition of inde-

pendent duchies and principalities until the eighteenth century.

Even in England and France, where feudal systems had gradually laid a foundation for the rise of strong monarchies, descendants of the feudal lords retained many privileges and special powers. Most new government offices—royal sheriffs and ministers, tax collectors and justices—were filled by noblemen. This was only practical, since most university students still came from noble families.

The dominance of the noble class in administering the royal government also made good financial sense. Despite the great migration to the cities during the High Middle Ages, the majority of Europeans still lived in rural villages. Rather than paying for full-time ministers, justices, tax collectors, and the like to serve every village and small town, it made better sense to assign these responsibilities to a local aristocrat. Such work usually amounted to only a part-time job, and many of the nobility could afford to fill these roles for little or no pay. Although they were now agents of the royal government, landholding noblemen thus continued to exert considerable influence on local affairs. Indeed, to the local peasant, it may have seemed as if little had changed.

The "Company," or Private Army

Similarly, rulers continued to rely on men of noble rank to recruit soldiers and raise armies. The great lords were still referred to as vassals of the king, but instead of recruiting soldiers as a condition of their feudal oath, noblemen now undertook

Vassal knights greet their returning lord. The feudal system of vassalage gave way to bureaucracies, but traces of the feudal social classes of royalty, nobility, and commoner have survived to this day.

this task for cash payments. In England a new term, "captain," was often used in place of "vassal." Each captain was usually responsible for raising his own "company" of soldiers, and he was paid according to the size of the company.

Although most of the soldiers who made up a company were mercenaries and not vassals, the company itself remained a kind of private army. The captain could contract his army to whomever he pleased. The document formalizing such an arrangement was called a military indenture. The following example of a military indenture was signed in 1416. It confirms the agreement of a Lord Hastings to provide soldiers to England's King Henry V for an overseas expedition. The indenture contract specifies the size and makeup of the army, the dates of service, and the wages the men are to be paid. Although it represents a new way to form armies, its concern for "booty" and "ransom of great lords" recalls the days of feudal warfare:

The said knights are retained by our lord the King to accompany him on expedition overseas which he will undertake in his own person, and there to serve him in war with nine men-at-arms (themselves included) and 18 archers well and suitably armed . . . for a quarter of a year beginning Monday the 22nd day of June. And each of the knights shall have two shillings a day, and each of the other men-at-arms one shilling a day, and each of the said archers half-a-shilling a day for their wages.

And concerning booty and capture of great lords for ransom . . . the king shall have the part which belongs to him according to the custom of ancient times.[38]

The Legacy of Feudalism

Thus, even as governmental and military bureaucracies grew, noblemen, the descendants of feudal lords, held a virtual monopoly on leadership in the military and in local governments. This tendency remained as late as World War I. The captains of the military in Europe were generally noblemen, and much as in the days of feudalism, their king called them to arms in moments of crisis. Likewise, the highest positions in the church were usually assigned to men of "noble blood."

Education remained one of the principal reasons for the continuing dominance of the noble class. Long after feudal armies and feudal oaths had become historical relics, noblemen continued to instill the ideals of chivalry in their children. In the Renaissance period, which immediately followed the High Middle Ages, these ideals were expanded to encompass the concept of the well-rounded gentleman, trained in riding and fencing, in history and the classics, and in the manners and social skills necessary for appreciating the refinements of life in the courts of great lords and ladies.

While the country gentlemen of eighteenth-century England, or the French courtiers of Louis XV, are far removed from the counts of Charlemagne, the warring knights of Normandy, or the bloodthirsty Crusaders, they are clearly descended from them. From the days of the German warlords until the early twentieth century, an elite class of soldiers persisted. Members of this class considered it their born privilege and duty to govern their fellow citizens and to command them on the field of battle. This is the legacy of feudalism.

Notes

Introduction: Feudalism: The Birth of the Middle Ages

1. Tactitus, *Germania,* quoted by Joseph Strayer, in *Feudalism.* Princeton, NJ: Van Nostrand, 1965.

Chapter 1: The First Kings

2. *Merovingian and Carolingian Formulas,* translated by K. Zeumer, quoted in Strayer, *Feudalism.*

3. *Merovingian and Carolingian Formulas,* quoted in Strayer, *Feudalism.*

4. *Annals of Charlemagne,* edited by Thomas Hodgkin, quoted in R. H. C. Davis, *A History of Medieval Europe,* 2nd ed. London: Longman Group, 1988.

5. Einhard, *Life of Charlemagne,* edited by James Bruce Ross and Mary Martin McLaughlin, in *The Portable Medieval Reader.* New York: Viking Press, 1949.

6. Einhard, *Life of Charlemagne.*

7. *Annals of Charlemagne,* edited by Hodgkin.

Chapter 2: From Soldiers to Noblemen: The Rise of Knights

8. *Annales Bertiniani,* edited by G. Waitz, quoted in Strayer, *Feudalism.*

9. *Annales Bertiniani,* quoted in Strayer, *Feudalism.*

10. *Annales Bertiniani,* quoted in Strayer, *Feudalism.*

11. Fulbert, bishop of Chartres, in *University of Pennsylvania Translations and Reprints,* edited by E. P. Cheyney, quoted in Brian Tierney, ed., *The Middle Ages,* Volume I: *Sources of Medieval History,* 4th ed. New York: Knopf, 1983.

12. Quoted in Robert Delort, *Life in the Middle Ages,* translated by Robert Allen. New York: Greenwich House, 1983.

Chapter 3: The Norman Triumph: Feudalism in England

13. F. Guizot, *History of France,* quoted in R. Allen Brown, *The Normans.* New York: St. Martin's Press, 1984.

14. *Anglo Saxon Chronicle,* quoted in Morris Bishop, *The Horizon Book of the Middle Ages.* New York: American Heritage, 1968.

15. *Anglo Saxon Chronicle,* quoted in Bishop, *The Horizon Book of the Middle Ages.*

16. *Anglo Saxon Chronicle,* quoted in Bishop, *The Horizon Book of the Middle Ages.*

17. *Anglo Saxon Chronicle,* quoted in Bishop, *The Horizon Book of the Middle Ages.*

Chapter 4: The Church as Feudal Lord

18. Pope Gregory VII, in John Neville Figgis, *Political Aspects of St. Augustine's City of God,* quoted in Will Durant, *The Story of Civilization,* Volume 4: *The Age of Faith.* New York: Simon & Schuster, 1950.

19. Pope Urban II, in Frederick A. Ogg, *A Source Book of Medieval History*. New York: American Book Company, 1907.

20. Urban II, in Ogg, *A Source Book of Medieval History*.

21. Urban II, in Ogg, *A Source Book of Medieval History*.

22. Urban II, in Ogg, *A Source Book of Medieval History*.

23. William of Malmesbury, "The Kings of England," in Ross and McLaughlin, *The Portable Medieval Reader*.

24. Raymond of Agiles, in Tierney, *The Middle Ages*, Volume I.

25. Bernard of Clairvaux, in T. A. Archer and C. L. Kingsford, *The Crusades*, quoted in Durant, *The Story of Civilization*, Volume 4.

26. *Chronicle of the Fourth Crusade*, quoted in Durant, *The Story of Civilization*, Volume 4.

Chapter 5: Feudalism and the Rise of Commerce

27. *Select Charters*, edited by W. Stubbs, quoted in Strayer, *Feudalism*.

28. *Actes des comtes de Flandre*, edited by F. Vercauteren, quoted in Strayer, *Feudalism*.

29. Frederick I, in *Ausgewählte Urkunden*, edited by W. Altmann and E. Bernheim, quoted in Strayer, *Feudalism*.

30. Du Cange, *Glossarium*, quoted in Strayer, *Feudalism*.

Chapter 6: The Decline of Feudal Power and the Rise of Kings

31. *Les très ancien Coutumier de Normandie*, edited by E. J. Tardif, quoted in Strayer, *Feudalism*.

32. Glanville, in *De legibus et consuetudinibus regni Angliae*, edited by George E. Woodbine, quoted in Strayer, *Feudalism*.

33. Henry II, quoted in Robert Fossier, *The Cambridge Illustrated History of the Middle Ages*, Volume 3, translated by Sarah Hanbury-Tennison. New York: Cambridge University Press, 1986.

Chapter 7: The Final Days of Feudalism

34. *Textes relatifs à l'histoire du Parlement*, quoted in Strayer, *Feudalism*.

35. *Layettes du Trésor des Chartres*, quoted in Strayer, *Feudalism*.

36. *Magna Carta*, in Ogg, *Source Book of Medieval History*.

37. Edward I, quoted by Sidney Painter, in *The Rise of the Feudal Monarchies*. Ithaca, NY: Cornell University Press, 1951.

38. John Malcolm William Bean, *Lord to Patron: Lordship in Late Medieval England*. Philadelphia: University of Pennsylvania Press, 1989.

Glossary

aid: Payment demanded from a vassal to help his lord cover the cost of a ransom payment or of a special circumstance, like the lord's son becoming a knight or his daughter marrying.

bailiff: (bailli) A great lord's chief administrator, who oversaw the administration of justice, taxation, and law enforcement within a specific district of an earldom, duchy, or county.

barbarian: Primitive or uncivilized.

baron: A term commonly used for a feudal lord.

benefice: A fief.

booty: Goods taken from the enemy in war.

bureaucrat: An appointed official.

caliph: Title taken by the heads of many Muslim states in northern Africa and the Near East.

chivalry: The values and customs of the knights of the High Middle Ages.

comitatus: An elite band of Germanic warriors.

commend: To submit oneself to the rule and protection of a lord.

count: The noble title given to the lord of a county.

county: A large region of a kingdom granted as a fief by a king to a powerful vassal. The holder of this fief bore the title of count.

courtier: An attendant in the court of a king or great lord.

danegeld: A general tax demanded by the English king. The tax was originally required to raise money to defend the kingdom from the Danes.

duchy: A large region of a kingdom granted as a fief by a king to a powerful vassal. Usually larger than a county. The holder of this fief bore the title of duke.

duke: The noble title given to the lord of a duchy.

earl: The title held by the majority of the highest ranking feudal lords in England.

envoy: Government representative.

excommunicate: Take away the right to take part in the rituals of the church, which were believed by many to be necessary for salvation.

fealty: A vassal's obligation to be loyal; homage.

feudalism: The economic system of private government and military organization based on feudal oaths between lords and vassals. In return for a promise of loyalty and military service, the lord granted his vassal a fief. Typically, the fief consisted of the right to hold and rule a piece of land.

feudal oath: The vow sworn by both lord and vassal to uphold the conditions of their agreement. The vassal swore his loyalty and promised military service, while the lord promised to honor and protect the vassal's fief.

fief: The fee that a lord granted to his vassal, usually in the form of land.

freeman: Anyone who was not a serf or a slave.

Gaul: The name given by the Romans to the area of Europe where France is now located.

heraldry: The use of symbolic pictures, or "coats of arms," to represent a noble family.

hereditary: Something that can be inherited.

hierarchy: A system with higher and lower ranks of power.

homage: A vassal's loyalty to his lord.

immunity: Free from another's rule or control.

indulgence: In the Roman Catholic church, freedom from the punishment due in purgatory for a sin.

investiture: The act of conferring a title or office on another.

knight: An elite mounted soldier. In the Middle Ages, being initiated into knighthood was reserved almost exclusively for noblemen.

lance: A long spear comprised of a steel spearhead attached to a long wooden stake.

liege: A vassal's primary feudal loyalty.

lord: The nobleman to whom a vassal swore his homage.

mace: A lead ball with sharp spikes, attached to a chain for swinging at the enemy.

mail: Pliable sheets of armor made from small steel links hooked together.

marquis: A noble title approximately equal to a duke.

medieval: Pertaining to the Middle Ages.

mercenary: A soldier that fights for anyone who will pay him.

military indenture: An agreement by a nobleman to provide a company of soldiers to his king in return for a specified payment.

nobility: The ruling class.

pilgrimage: A journey to a religious shrine.

precarium: A fief that was not hereditary. When the vassal who held a precarium died, the fief was returned to his lord.

primogeniture: The right of the oldest child, especially a son, to inherit a parent's entire estate.

relief: The payment a new vassal had to make to his lord for the right to inherit a fief.

romance: A long story about the deeds of a heroic knight.

scepter: A rod or staff held by a ruler as a symbol of his power.

scutage: A payment made by a vassal to his lord in place of his military service.

secular: Non-religious.

sepulcher: Tomb.

sheriff: A local government official in England who was a representative of the king.

shire: A royal government district in England administered by a sheriff, who was a representative of the king.

siege: To surround a castle or city with the intent of capturing it.

squire: A knight's right-hand assistant, usually someone training for the knighthood himself.

subinfeudate: To divide a fief into smaller fiefs.

thane: The vassal of an earl in Anglo-Saxon England before the Norman conquest.

tithe: A gift to the church equal to one-tenth of one's earnings.

tribute: A payment made by a peasant to his lord, often in goods rather than money.

troubadour: Poets who wrote and sang poems and ballads of love and knighthood.

vassal: A nobleman who swore homage to another nobleman became that nobleman's vassal.

verdict: The decision made by a jury in a court of law.

ward: A person or place under special care or guardianship.

For Further Reading

R. Allen Brown, *The Normans*. New York: St. Martin's Press, 1984. An in-depth history of Norman civilization and the great Norman conquests. Includes photographs and reprints of medieval artifacts.

Mike Corbiskey, *The Middle Ages*. New York: Facts on File, 1990. Maps, charts, illustrations, and text explore the history and culture of the Middle Ages.

Robert Delort, *Life in the Middle Ages*, translated by Robert Allen. New York: Greenwich House, 1983. A thorough, richly illustrated cultural history of the Middle Ages, depicting the life-styles of peasants, the nobility, and the men and women of the church.

David Edge and John Miles Paddock, *Arms and Armor of the Medieval Knight*. New York: Crescent Books, 1988. A history of knights from their barbarian and Roman beginnings through the sixteenth century. With an abundance of photographs of authentic armor and weapons, this book presents an interesting perspective on medieval history. Includes a glossary.

Fiona MacDonald, *Everyday Life: The Middle Ages*. Morristown, NJ: Silver Burdett, 1986. Describes in text and illustrations how people in Europe lived and worked between 1200 and 1500. Includes glossary and tables of important events and famous people.

Antoine Sabbagh, *Europe in the Middle Ages*, translated by Anthea Ridett. Morristown, NJ: Silver Burdett, 1986. Describes in text and illustrations the history of Europe during the Middle Ages with emphasis on the social, political, and cultural developments and changes.

Gloria Verges, *Journey Through History: The Middle Ages*, translated by Jean Grasso Fitzpatrick. Hauppage, NY: Barron's Educational Series, 1988. An illustrated history of the Middle Ages with a fictional story involving children to depict the time in history.

Martin Windrow, *The Medieval Knight*. New York: Franklin Watts, 1985. An illustrated portrayal of the training, weapons, and life-style of a typical medieval knight, with glossary and timeline.

Works Consulted

John Malcolm William Bean, *From Lord to Patron: Lordship in Late Medieval England.* Philadelphia: University of Pennsylvania Press, 1989. Part of the *Middle Ages* series, this work contains a wealth of primary sources of feudal and indenture contracts; traces the gradual shift from private feudal armies to mercenary armies and indentured military service in England.

Morris Bishop, *The Horizon Book of the Middle Ages.* New York: American Heritage, 1968. A thorough overview of the cultural, political, and intellectual history of the Middle Ages. Filled with photographs and reprints of medieval artifacts.

Marc Bloch, *Feudal Society,* translated by L. A. Manyon. Chicago: University of Chicago Press, 1961. A scholarly history of the political and social organization of medieval France that arose from a feudal economy and military system.

R. Allen Brown, *The Normans.* New York: St. Martin's Press, 1984. An in-depth history of the Norman civilization and the great Norman conquests. Includes photographs and reprints of medieval artifacts.

Peter R. Coss, *Lordship, Knighthood, and Locality: A Study in English Society from 1180 to 1280.* New York: Cambridge University Press, 1991. Uses historical records from Coventry Abbey to portray social and political conditions of the Norman nobility in England.

J. S. Critchley, *Feudalism.* Boston: Allen & Unwin, 1978. A comparative study of feudal societies throughout the world in various historical periods.

Joseph Dahmus, ed., *Seven Medieval Histories.* Chicago: Nelson-Hall, 1982. A collection of seven of the best known medieval chronicles: Procopius, Bede, Al-Tabari, Otto of Freising, Matthew Paris, John Froissart, and Ibn Khaldun.

R. H. C. Davis, *A History of Medieval Europe,* 2nd ed. London: Longman Group, 1988. Excellent history of early medieval period up to the Viking invasions. Includes maps and chronology of important events.

Robert Delort, *Life in the Middle Ages,* translated by Robert Allen. New York: Greenwich House, 1983. A thorough, richly illustrated cultural history of the Middle Ages, depicting the life-styles of peasants, the nobility, and the men and women of the church.

Will Durant, *The Story of Civilization,* Volume 4: *The Age of Faith.* New York: Simon & Schuster, 1950. A lively and exhaustive history of medieval Europe and the Near East from the decline of the Roman Empire in the fourth century to the end of the Middle Ages, or approximately 1300. Extremely useful chronological tables.

David Edge and John Miles Paddock, *Arms and Armor of the Medieval Knight.* New York: Crescent Books, 1988. A history of knights from their barbarian and Roman beginnings through the sixteenth century. With an abundance of photographs of authentic armor and weapons, this book presents an interesting perspective on medieval history. Includes a glossary.

Robert Fossier, *The Cambridge Illustrated History of the Middle Ages,* Volume 3, translated by Sarah Hanbury-Tennison. New

York: Cambridge University Press, 1986. Part of a three-volume series on the history of the Middle Ages, Fossier's book may well be the best documented, best illustrated, and most thorough overview of the late Middle Ages available.

Robert Fossier, *The Life of William the Marshal.* New York: Cambridge University Press, 1983.

Frederick A. Ogg, ed., *A Source Book of Medieval History.* New York: American Book Company, 1907.

Sidney Painter, *The Rise of the Feudal Monarchies.* Ithaca, NY: Cornell University Press, 1951. Part of the series, *The Development of Western Civilization,* this book provides a lucid account of the constant struggle among monarchs, barons, and the church in France, England, and Germany from the time of Charlemagne to the end of the thirteenth century. Includes a chronology.

Jean-Pierre Poly, *The Feudal Transformation: 900–1200,* translated by Caroline Higgitt. New York: Holmes and Meier, 1991. A revisionist's account of feudal anarchy in France during the early years of the Capetian dynasty, covering the invasions of Norsemen and Saracens and the gradual emergence of a strong monarchy under Louis VI.

James Bruce Ross and Mary Martin McLaughlin, eds., *The Portable Medieval Reader.* New York: Viking Press, 1949. This volume is one of the most comprehensive collections of medieval letters and essays ever compiled. It encompasses European politics, warfare, religion, philosophy, science, and the arts from 1050 to 1500 and includes a chronological table for that period.

Carl Stephenson, *Medieval Feudalism.* Ithaca, NY: Great Seal Books, 1956. A definitive study of feudalism as a unique political and economic system that developed in northern Europe, especially after the dissolution of Charlemagne's empire.

Joseph R. Strayer, *Feudalism.* Princeton, NJ: Van Nostrand, 1965. Part I is an introduction to feudalism in medieval Europe and an overview of the evolution of the institution from its Germanic and Roman origins to a full-fledged political system. Part II is an excellent collection of readings from primary sources.

Brian Tierney, ed., *The Middle Ages,* Volume I: *Sources of Medieval History,* 4th ed. New York: Knopf, 1983. A very readable chronological collection of the writings of medieval historians, from the decline of the Roman Empire in the fifth century to the time of Chaucer in the late fourteenth century.

Index

Picture Credits

About the Author

Timothy Levi Biel was born and raised in eastern Montana. A graduate of Rocky Mountain College, he received a Ph.D. in literary studies from Washington State University. He is currently teaching in the communications department of the University of Texas at Arlington.

He is the author of numerous nonfiction books, many of which are part of the highly acclaimed Zoobooks series for young readers. In addition, he has written *The Black Death: World Disasters,* and several other books for Lucent Books.